A GIFT

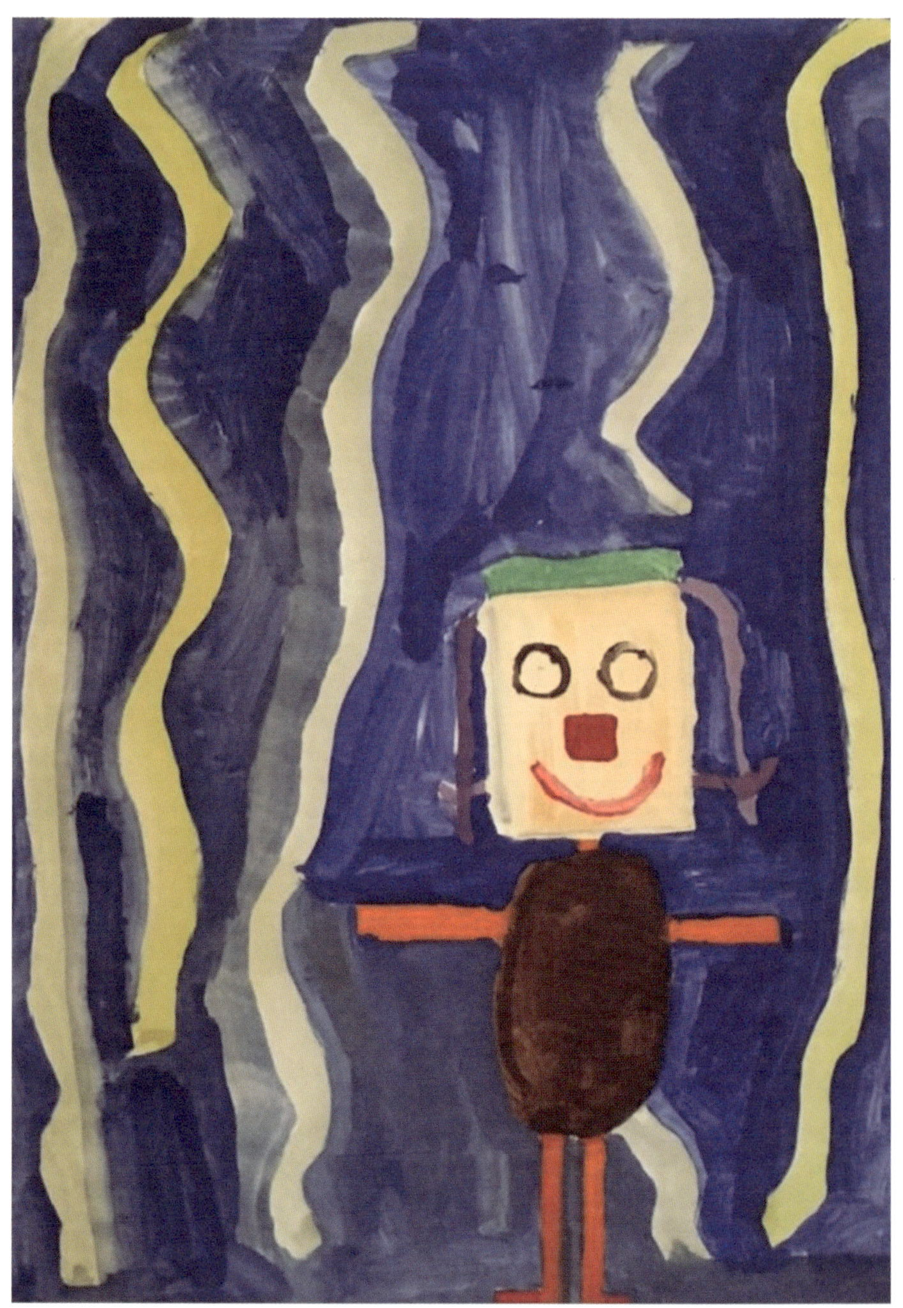

The Robot Carnival, Katrin, aged 9, Germany. Courtesy The Little Museum of Modern Art

A GIFT

from artists, photographers and poets (under 13)

edited by julian rothenstein

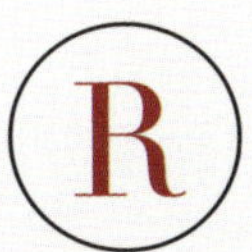

A REDSTONE BOOK

First published in 2022
Redstone Press, 7a St Lawrence Terrace, London W10 5SU
email: redstone.press@gmail.com website: www.theredstoneshop.com

ISBN 978-0-9955181-3-1

Design: Julian Rothenstein
Artwork: Tom Baxter / Production: Geoff Barlow
Printed and bound in China by 1010 Printing International Ltd

Many of the works in this book were found on Instagram or Pinterest. Every effort has been made to trace contributors but in many cases this was impossible. If application is made in writing to the publisher, any omissions will be included in future editions.

From *Miracles: Poems by Children of the English-speaking world*. Richard Lewis ed.
Reprinted by permission of Simon and Schuster:
page 28: Peter Kelso, *Poems* / page 90: Deborah Ensign, *Mirror, Mirror* / page 40: Karen Crawford, *Being Nobody* / page 50: Brian Andrews, *The Doors* / Annabel Laurance, *My Brain*

From *There Are Two Lives: Poems by Children of Japan*, Richard Lewis ed.
Reprinted by permission of Simon and Schuster:
page 24 Sakai Akiko, *Mountains* / page 27: Kuroda Sadahiro, *Teacher's Jacket*

Thanks to: Zoe Barton, Charles Boyle, Steve Feldman, Tom Gatti, Rhiannon Gooding, Leo Hollis, Natalie Hume, Hiang Kee, Max Porter, David Shrigley, Calum Storrie, Carey Young.

Poetry Box, New Zealand
This online poetry page for children is run by Paula Green who has written numerous books for children and is herself a poet.

Children's Museum of the Arts, New York
This organisation holds a large collection of works painted by children during the Great Depression in the 1930s. The Federal Art Project was a government-sponsored programme which provided free art classes to children and adults at more than 100 centres created under the intiative.

The Cyrene Mission, Zimbabwe (formerly Rhodesia)
This agricultural school was founded in 1939. Art classes were mandatory and works by schoolchildren taught by the school's founder Edward Paterson are much prized.

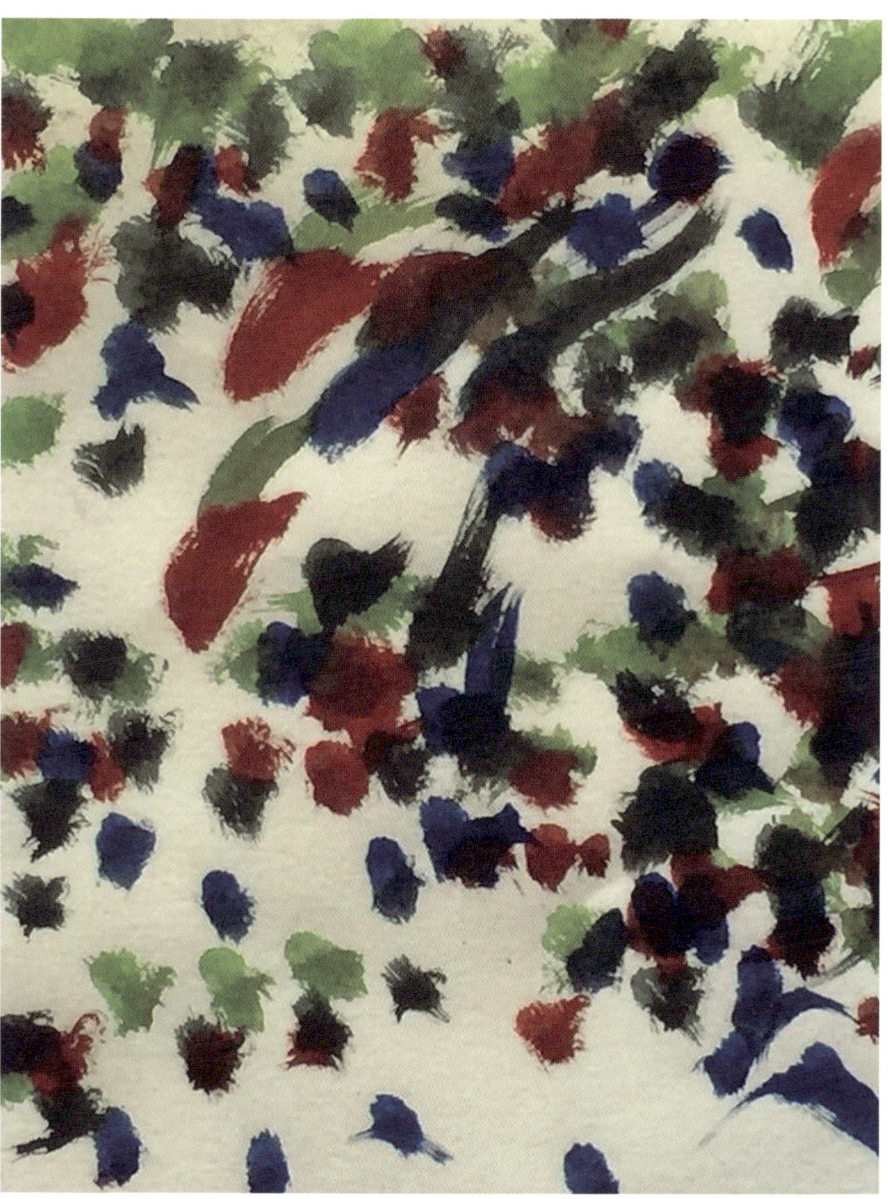

Unknown artist

wondering 17

feeling 35

messaging 53

playing 83

looking 117

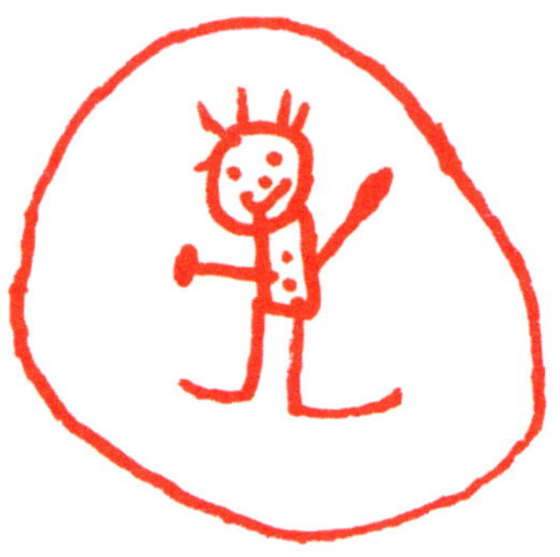

Boy inside a hard boiled egg, by a boy aged 6

WONDERING

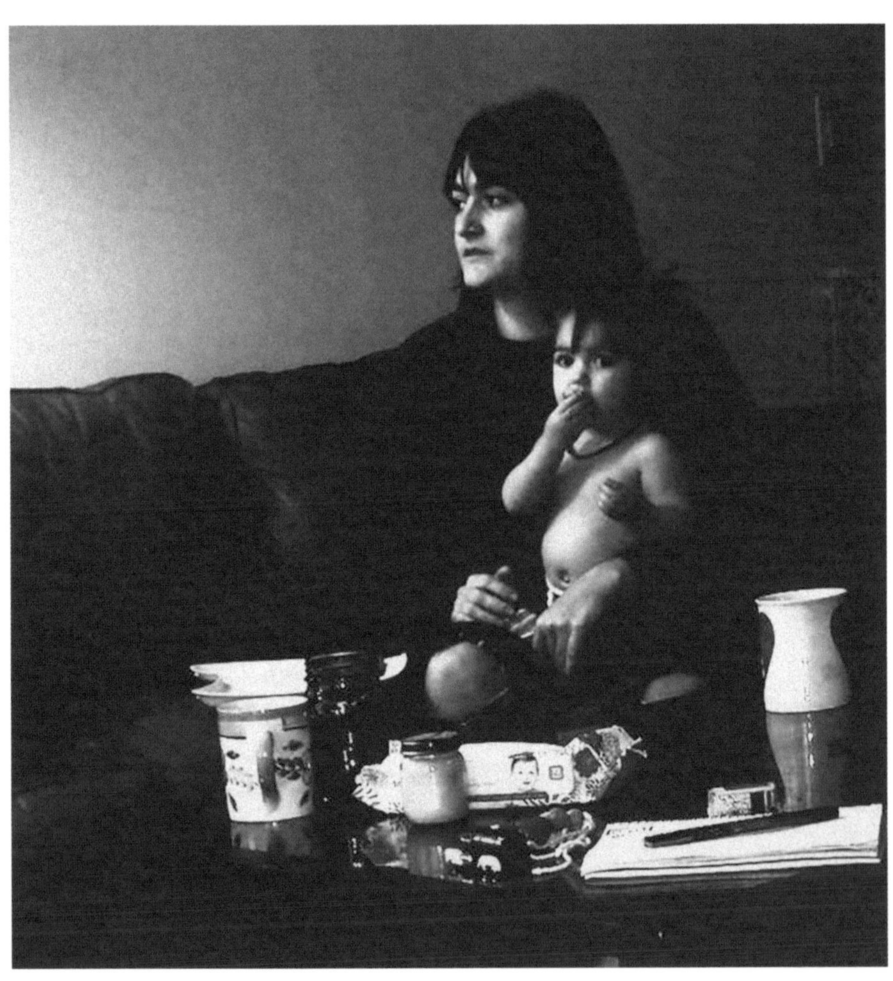

Photo by unknown photographer, aged 4

WONDER

Wonder comes to us, creeping into our heads.
Adults throw wonder away, like a moth-eaten blanket.
But children treasure it.
Children see race car boxes, and lava floors.
Children see the magic in the air.
That's why they make friends wherever they go.
Why they are so happy.
They see the awesomeness in everything.
So when you have a little time, let in the wonder.
If we could all stop a moment, and try
to see the world through a child's point of view, our
worlds will be happier.
So put a smile on your face, and wonder.

Paige Layton, aged 10, New Zealand. Courtesy Poetry Box

WONDER

I wonder what school was years ago.
Once, they might've carved writings on rocks,
Or they might have jumped about on logs for exercise.
They probably wanted to fly like birds, soaring in the sky.
I think some children travelled, maybe by horse?

Carolyn Xiao, aged 9, New Zealand. Courtesy Poetry Box

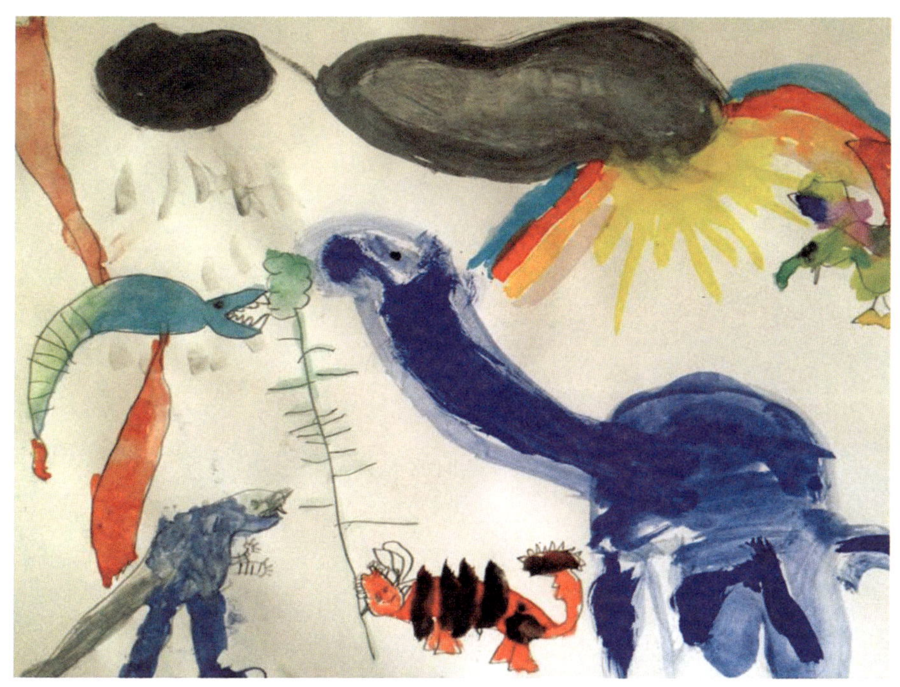

Tyrannosaurus, Triceratops, Brachiosaurus and Two Flying Dinosaurs, Bela, aged 4, Germany. Courtesy The Little Museum of Modern Art

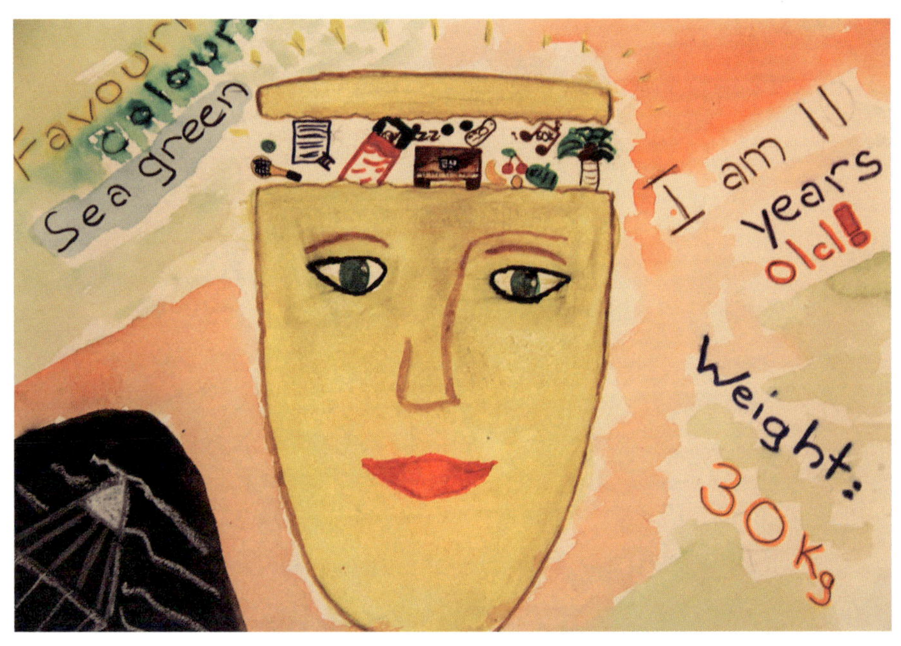

Unknown artist. Courtesy of the Permanent Collection of Children's Museum of the Arts

JUST WONDERING

I wonder
If on the Tundra
You need an bandana
Like on the Savannah?

Gemma Lovewell, aged 11, New Zealand
Courtesy Poetry Box

MOUNTAINS

Mountains
have nerves.
The roots of the trees
are the nerves of the mountains.
Mountains have ears.
They copy what man says.
Everybody calls it
echoes.

Sakai Akiko, aged 7, Japan

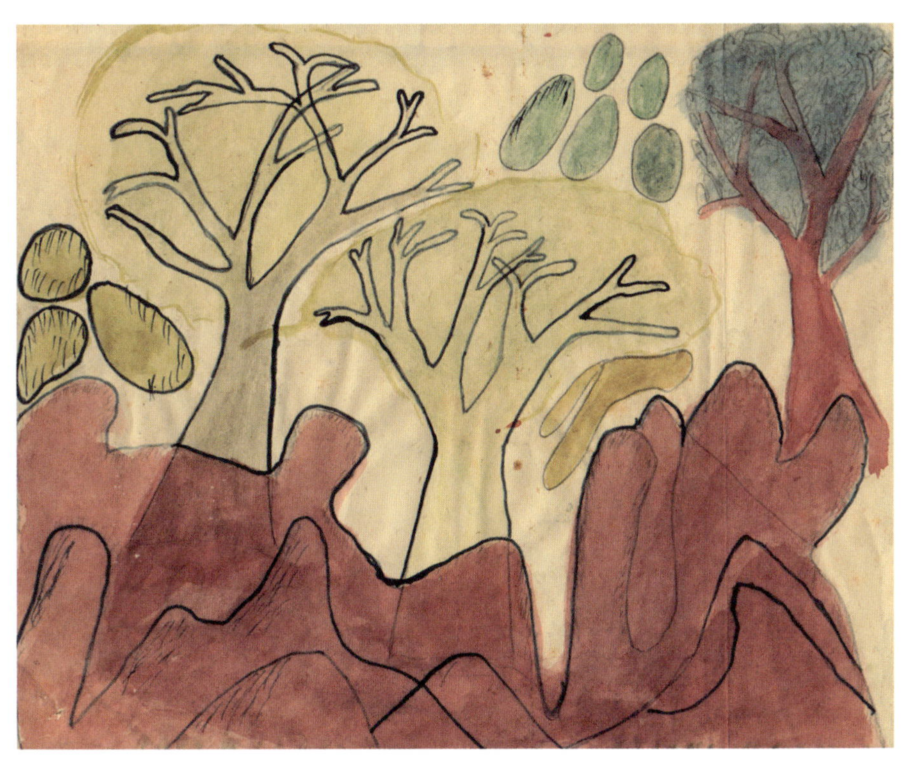

Unknown artist, South Africa, c.1940. From the Cyrene Mission, Zimbabwe

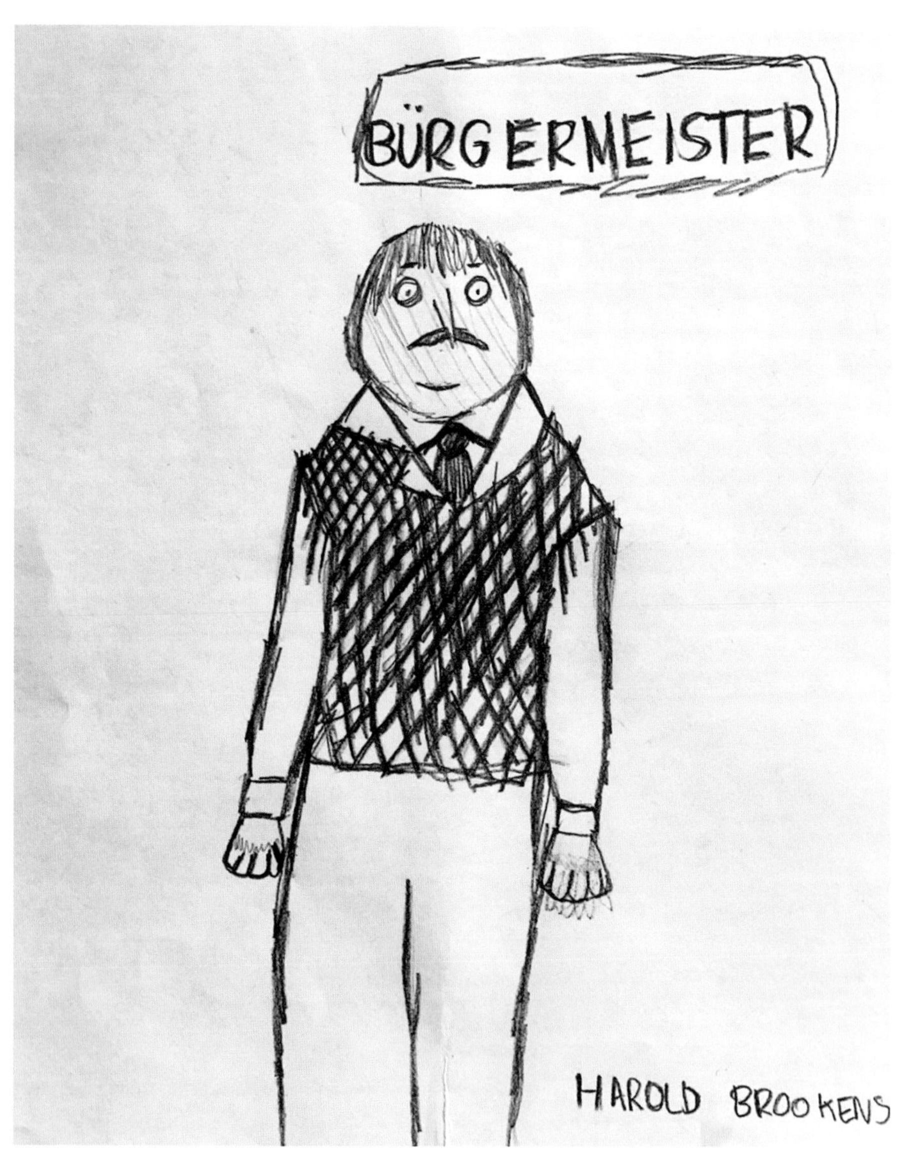

Wilhelmine von Stauffenberg, aged 9, Germany

TEACHER'S JACKET

Our teacher told us about poems
Whenever he spoke a word
he straightened his jacket
or buttoned it up.
He was nervous about his jacket.
It was annoying to see him so restless.
I almost wondered if he was a bit crazy.

Kuroda Sadahiro, aged 10, Japan

THE TEACHER

Constantly talking moaning grumbling
He works the day through impulsive
Like a droning bee, a line of sighs.

Matthew, aged 8, UK

POEMS

In poems, our earth's wonders
Are windowed through
      Words

A good poem must haunt the heart
And be heeded by the head of the
      Hearer

With a wave of words, a poet can
Change his feelings into cool, magical, mysterious
      Miracles

Without poetry our world would be
Locked within itself – no longer enchanted by the poet's
      Spell

Peter Kelso, aged 11, Australia

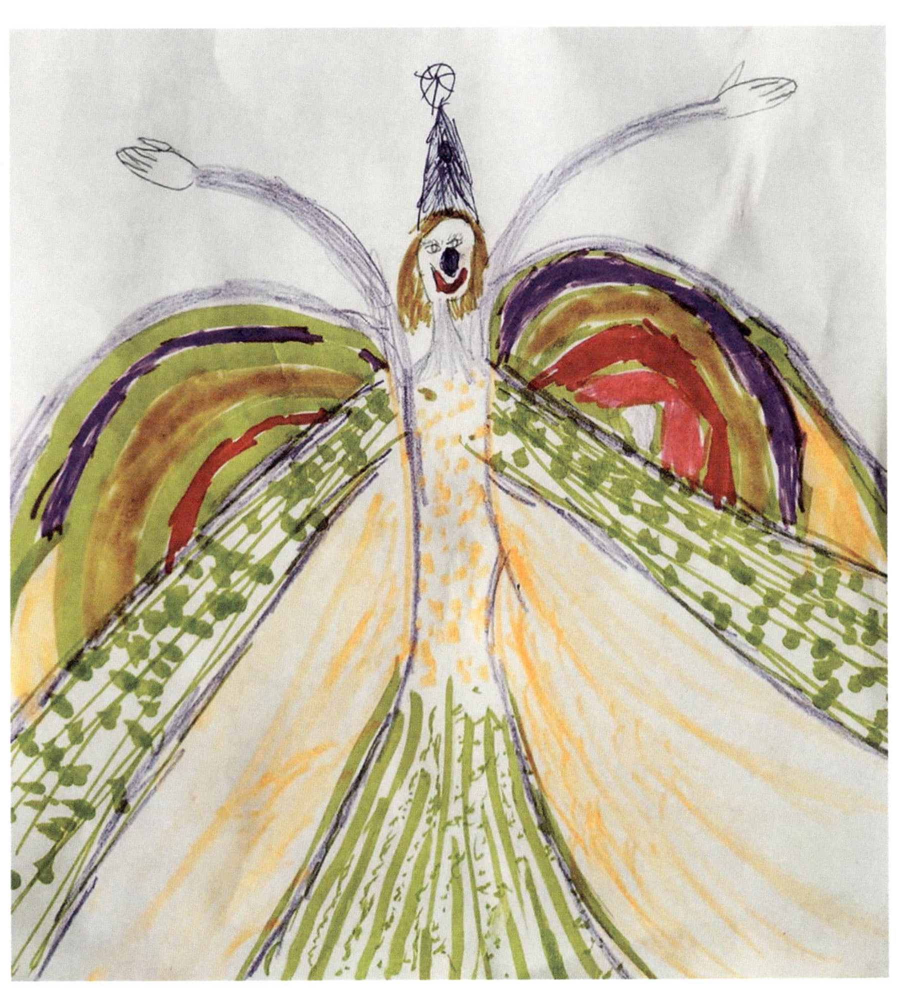

Anna, aged 7, Poland

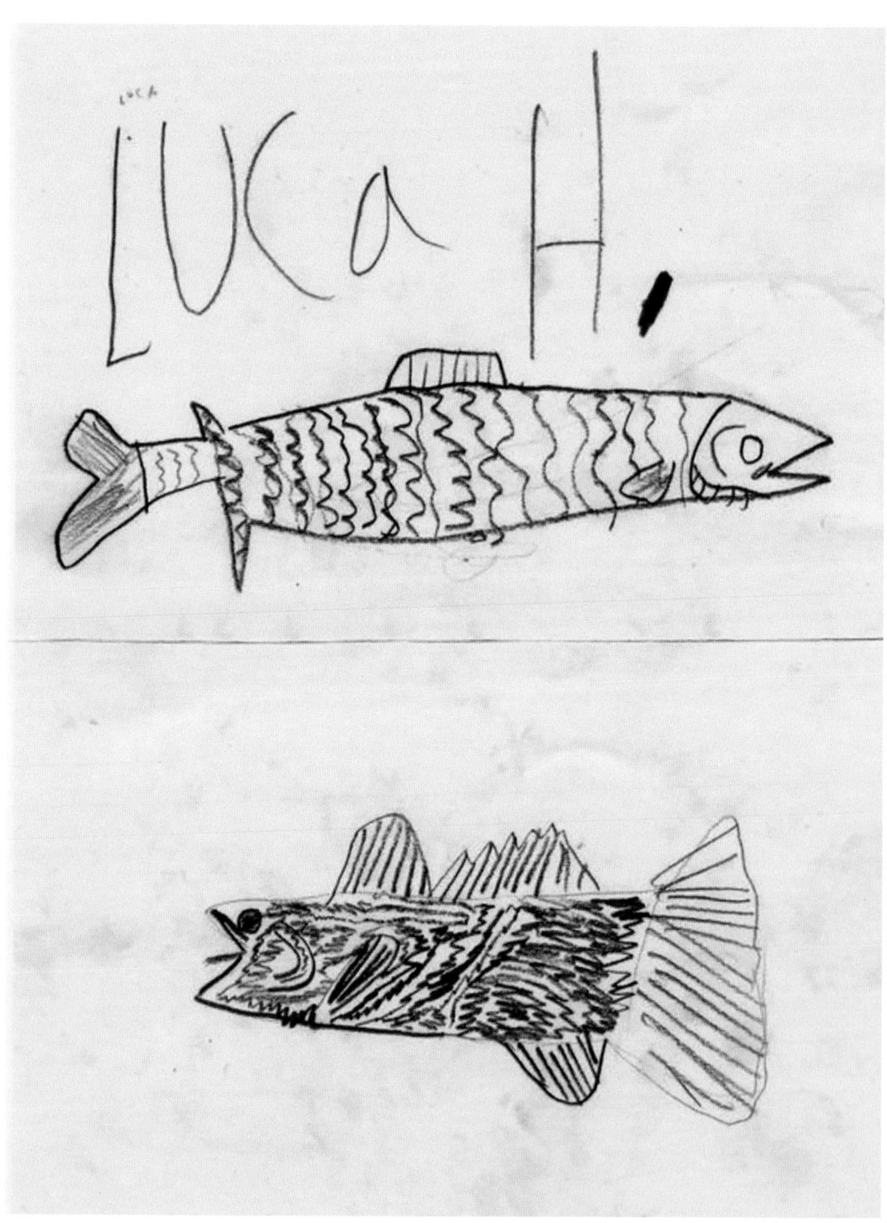

Luca H., age unknown, USA. Courtesy of the Permanent Collection of Children's Museum of the Arts

WONDER

I wonder about Antarctica
the polar bears start disappearing
Penguins are losing hope
Ice melts away and sea levels rise
Fish are slipping away into darkness

Isabelle Harrison, aged 8, New Zealand
courtesy Poetry Box

A QUESTIONNAIRE

Do you ever talk to yourself? And, if so, what do you talk about?
Describe your perfect day. Describe the last dream that you had.
What is your biggest worry? What is your perfect day?

I talk to myself in the night, I say – when will my dragon be here?
I worry about my dragon being hurt in a storm.
(Ruben, aged 4)

I talk to myself to be very good.
On my best day I want it to be sunny and I would see my grandma because she's far away, like a billion miles away or something. (Agata, aged 5)

I don't talk to myself ever. (Ryder, aged 5)

When I was talking to myself is when I was counting the days until my birthday. (Nirvana, aged 6)

My perfect day was in summer: my dad splashed me with water.
(Luca, aged 6)

I talk to myself about when I was hoping to have a perfect parent-teacher meeting. (Edie, aged 6)

On my perfect day I would look at the sky for 24 hours.
I dream about looking at the floor. (Liam, aged 8)

My dream is that I could fly all over the houses and that I was a real princess and everyone will say that I am truly a wonderful girl of the town. (Claire, aged 6)

My dream starts by me having a wonderful sleep in and when I wake up I have a delicious breakfast and invite my 10 friends over to play with my 3 cats. Then we will go to the movies and watch *Sing 2* and eat rainbow popcorn and sweets. When we get home we will find out that covid and racism is over. (Sofia, aged 8)

Responses from children at Colville Primary School in west London, with thanks to Zoe Barton, assistant head teacher.

FEELING

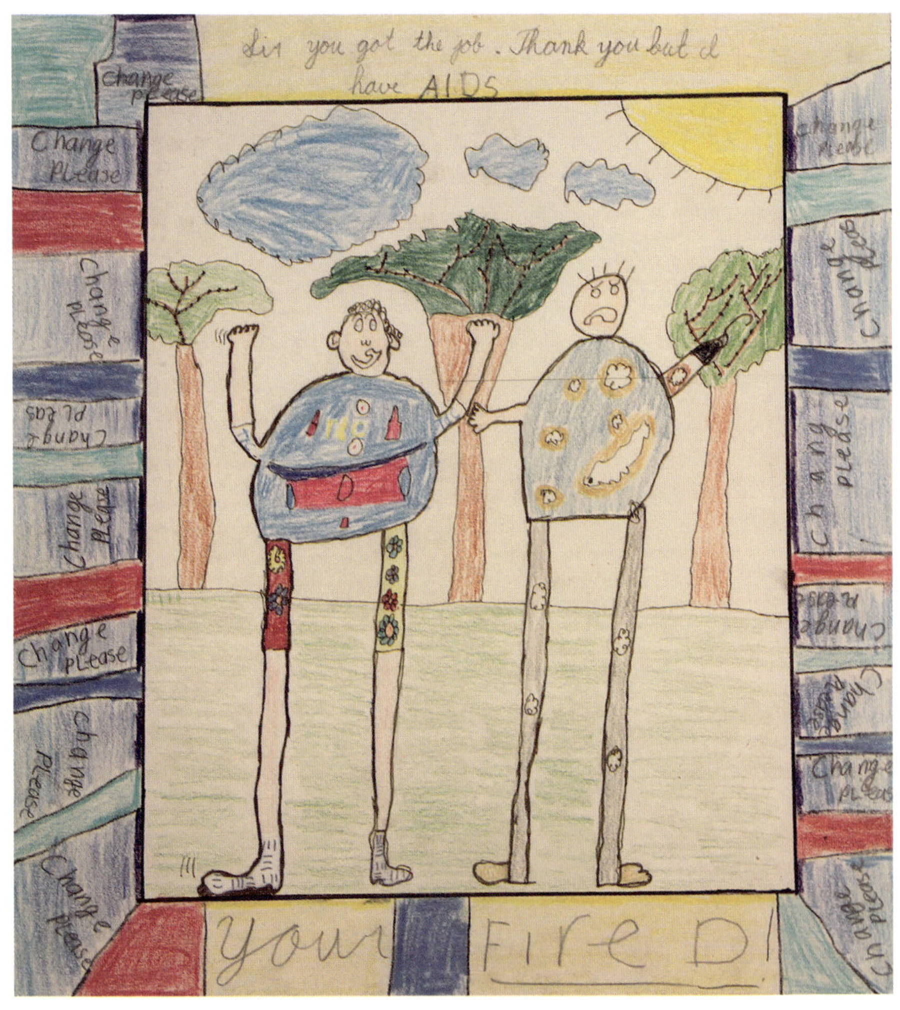

Caroline Conners, aged 12, USA. Courtesy of the Permanent Collection of Children's Museum of the Arts

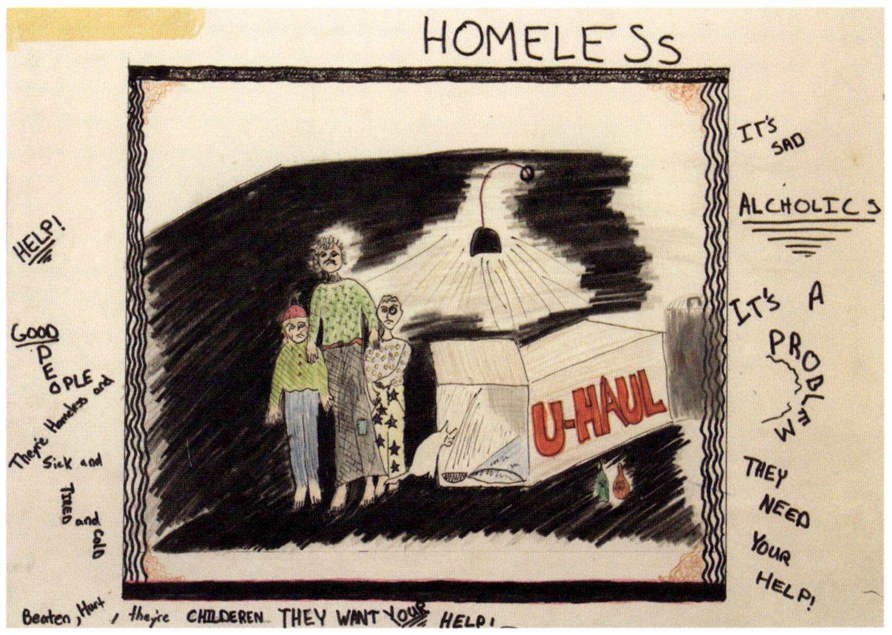

Kate Mellin, aged 12, USA. Courtesy of the Permanent Collection of Children's Museum of the Arts

No-one should have to live in the street

Statement by Tom, aged 8, USA

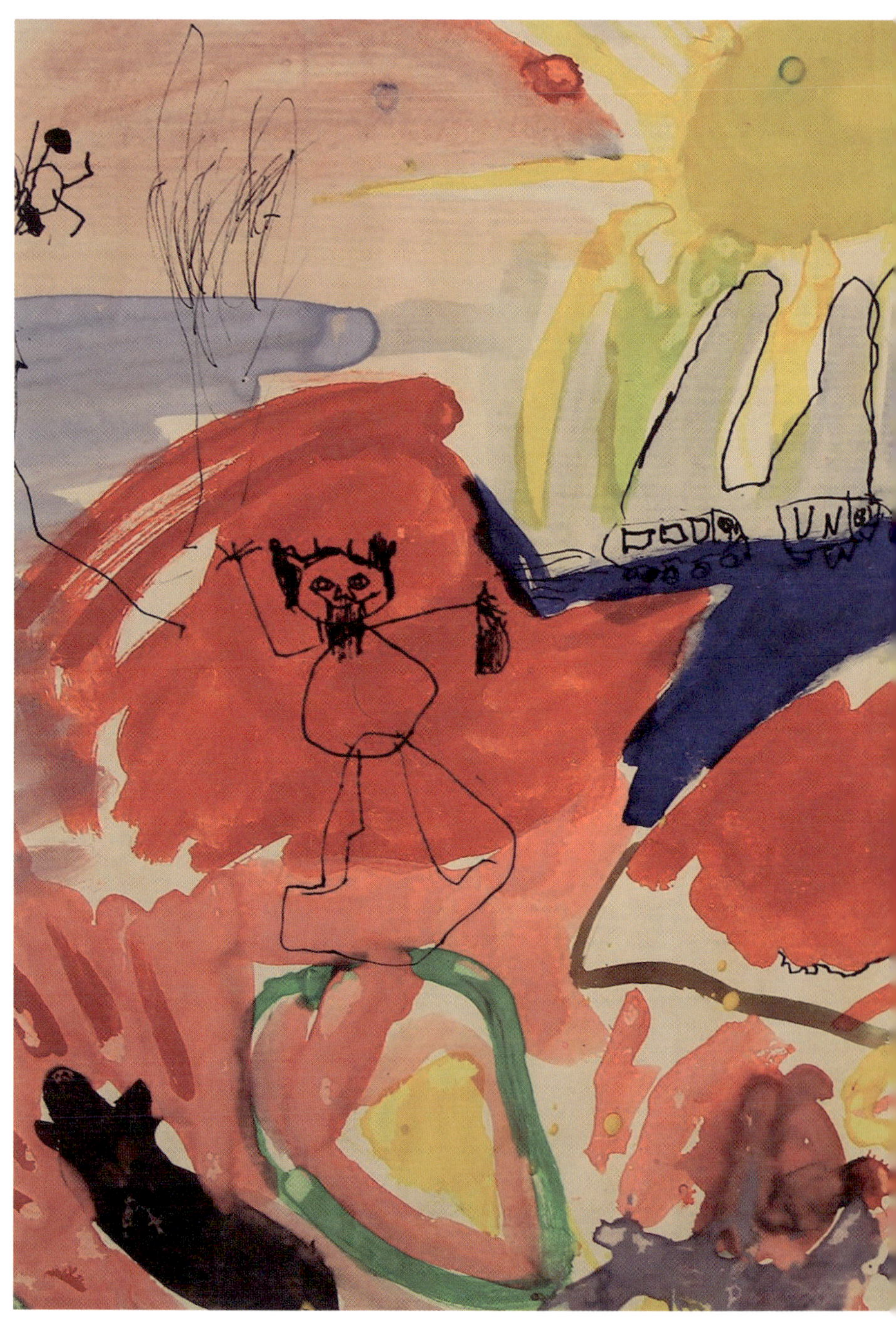

The Princess Who Was Afraid of the Beast, Emilie, aged 5, Denmark. Courtesy of the Permanent Collection of Children's Museum of the Arts

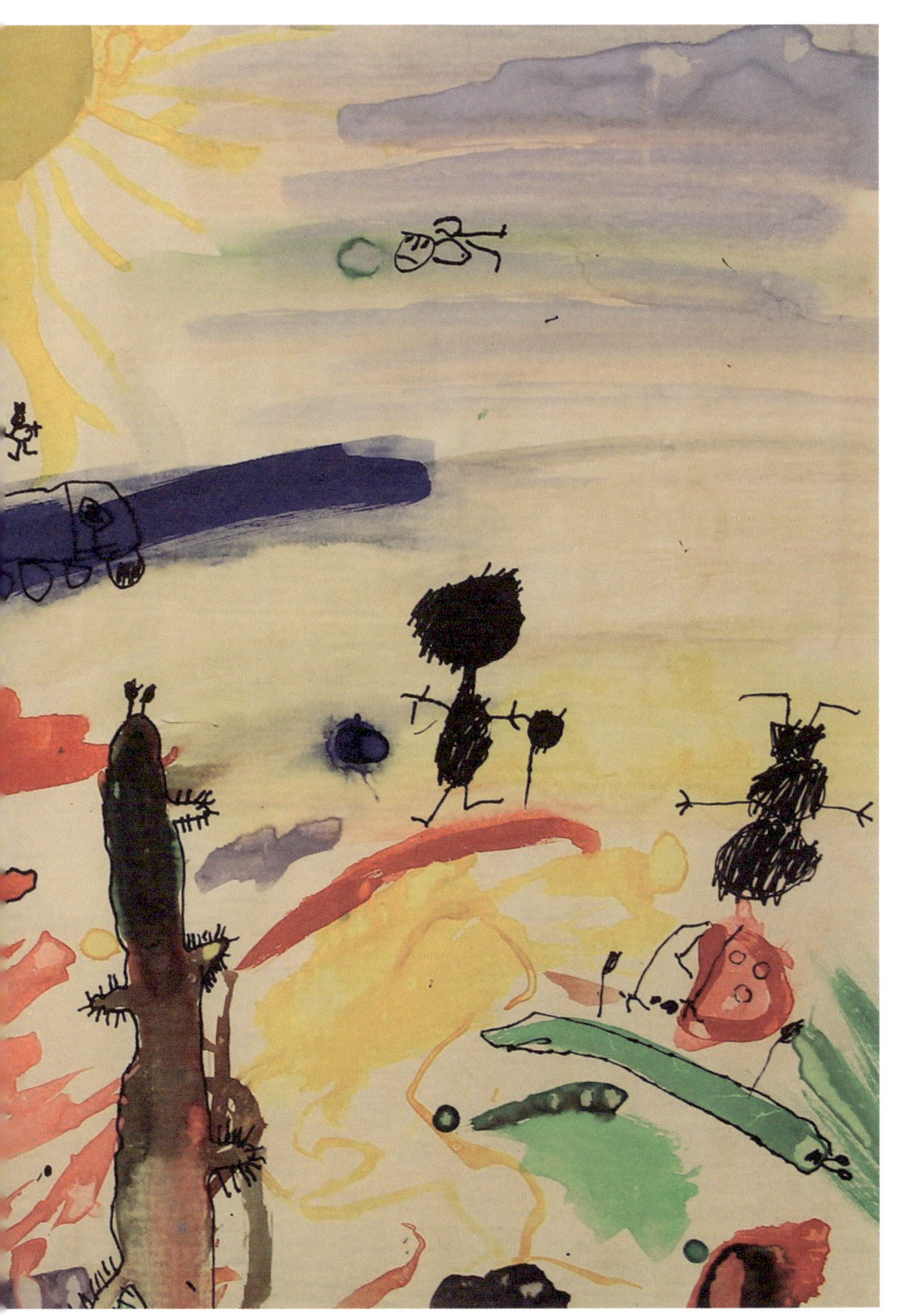

BEING NOBODY

Have you ever felt like nobody?
Just a tiny speck of air.
When everyone's around you,
And you are just not there.

Karen Crawford, aged 9, USA

I WISH TO GOD HE'D TELL ME WHO HE IS

This poem
Like many I call my own
Was in fact written by an anonymous little man
Who stands behind me and takes hold of my pencil
Over my shoulder

I never turn around until I'm sure he's gone away
Because I'm terrified
That he wears a bowler hat
Carries a briefcase
And works from nine to five
Putting words into the mouths of upstarts
Who call themselves writers

Sarah Gilbert, aged 12, UK

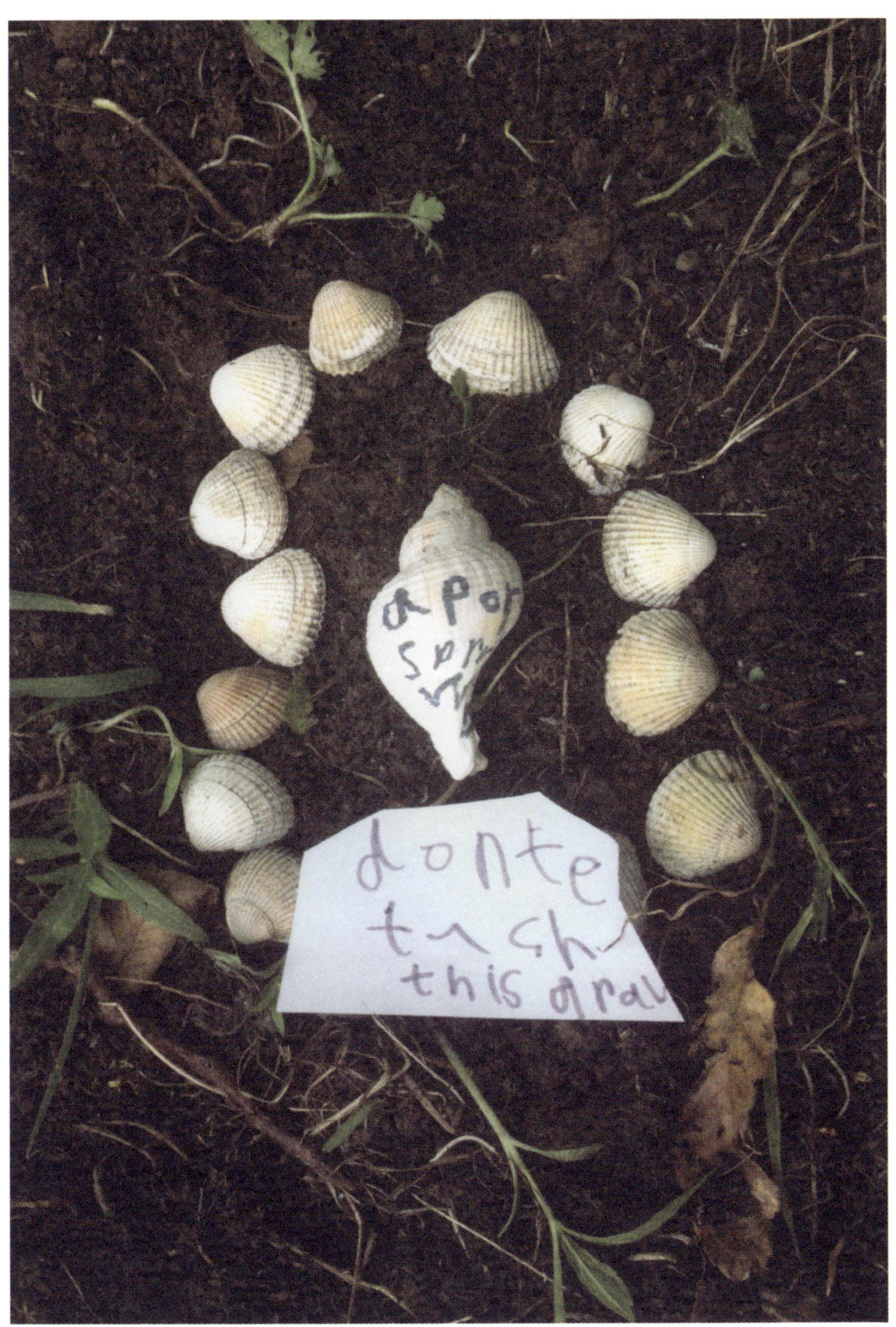

A Por Sparrow, Oriel Gooding, aged 4, UK. The legend reads: *don't touch this grave*

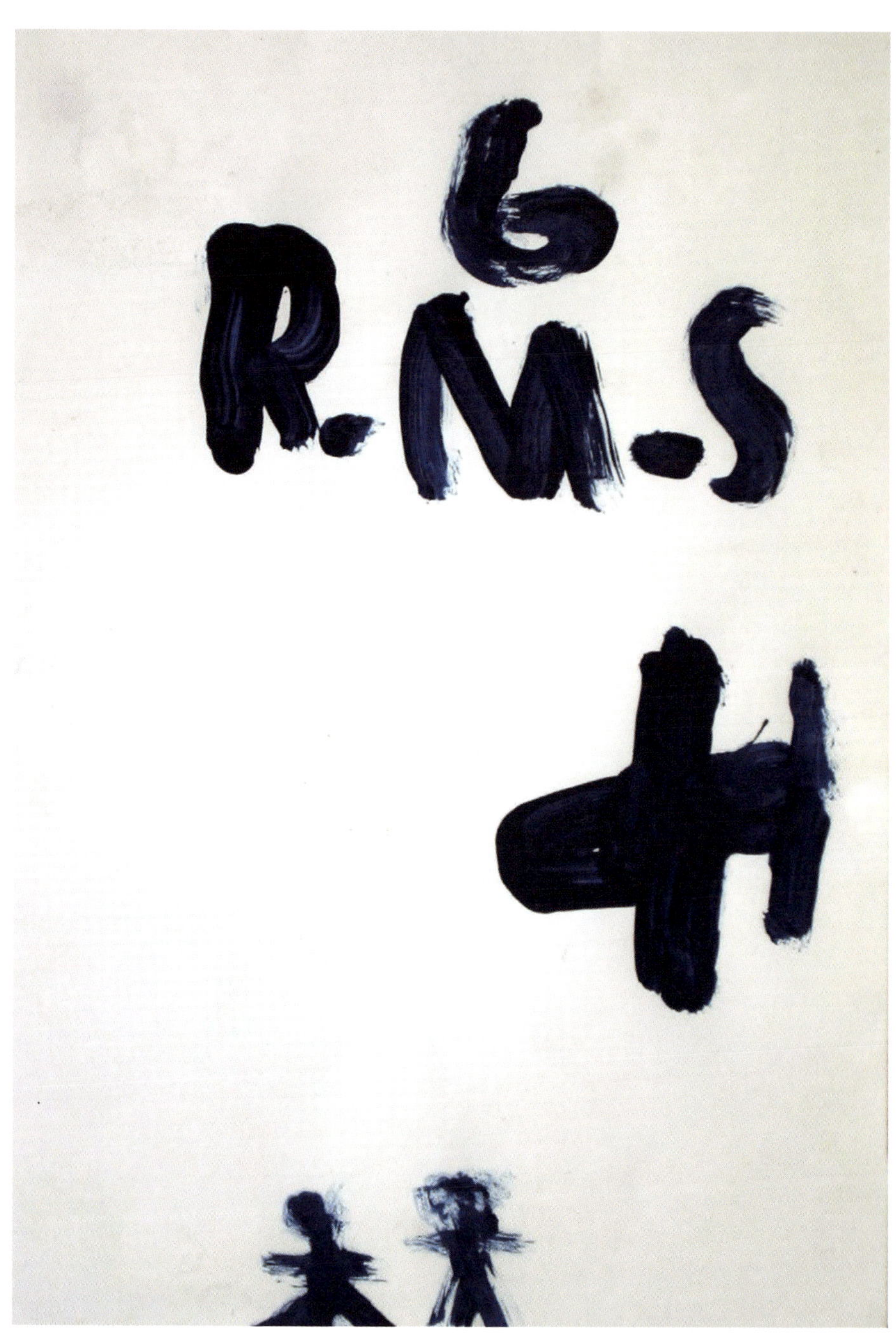

Unknown artist. Courtesy of the Permanent Collection of Children's Museum of the Arts, 9/11 Collection

IF ONLY

If only all the dead could cry out in a single roar

To say don't send another son

To give his life to war.

They'd say look at how we lay,

Without life or limb

The bullet that tore our hearts apart

Has caused our eyes to dim.

The orders are the same,

Move forward boys, make haste

Just put your mind to the task

Don't think of the horror and waste

The war boys, the war is for all!

God is on the side that's right.

But the devil owns the battlefield

When you hear the cries at night.

If only all the dead could cry out in a single roar

To say don't send another son

To give his life to war.

Kristen, aged 8, New Zealand. Courtesy Poetry Box

from LAMENT FROM SYRIA

Can anyone teach me
how to make a homeland?
Heartfelt thanks if you can,
heartiest thanks,
from the house-sparrows,
the apple-trees of Syria,
and yours very sincerely.

Amineh Abou Kerech, aged 13, Syria

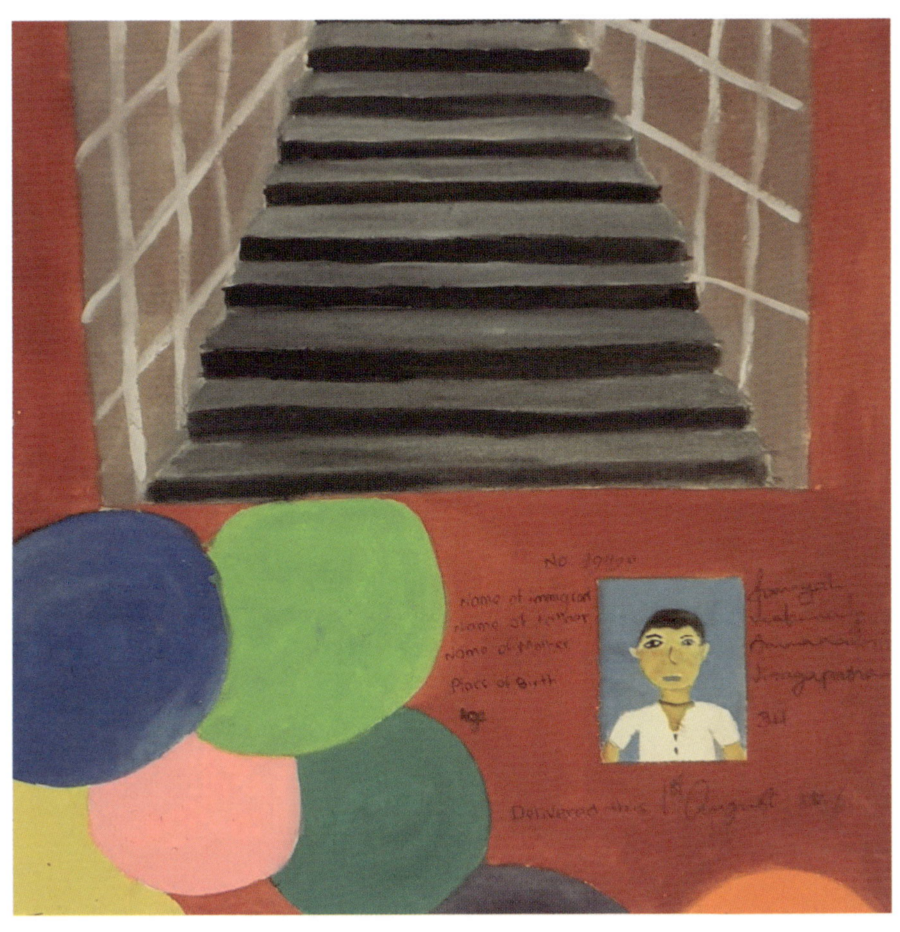

Aapravasi Ghat (the port where Indian immigrants first landed in Mauritius), Tanushree Chinnia, aged 12, Mauritius. Courtesy Unesco.

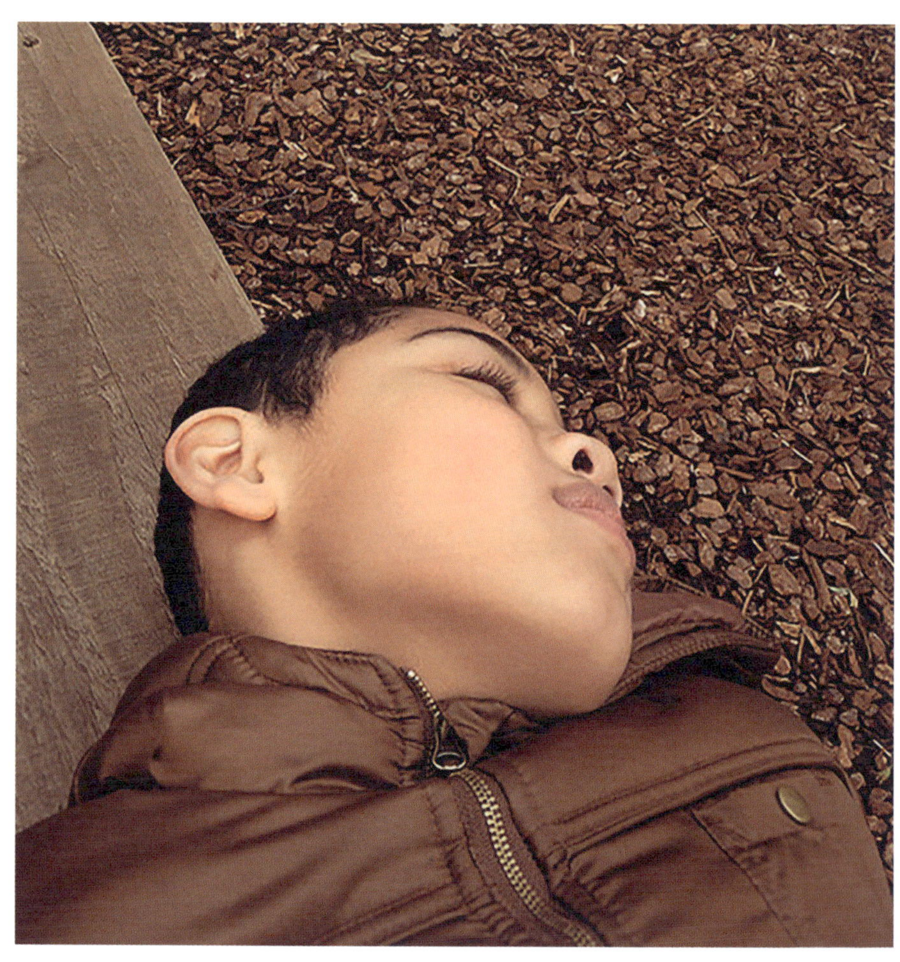

Photo by Aaron, aged 10, UK. Courtesy Cubitt Artists

TOBY

Let's doodle round the holes in our paper
and tap patterns into the silence.
I want to tell you the story
of why we should get a round of applause
for smiling when it doesn't go with our outfits
or your slappable face.
You make me want to condition your hair
at 1.22 am. You make me want to run through trains
and whistle with braces and pick up the sun,
pat it dry, and hand it to you.
I've never not worried about you,
the way fears won't stain your orange peel cheeks
scares me.
You make me want to smell
the miscellaneous clouds
in the weight of the words you gave me.

Edie Michael, aged 13, UK

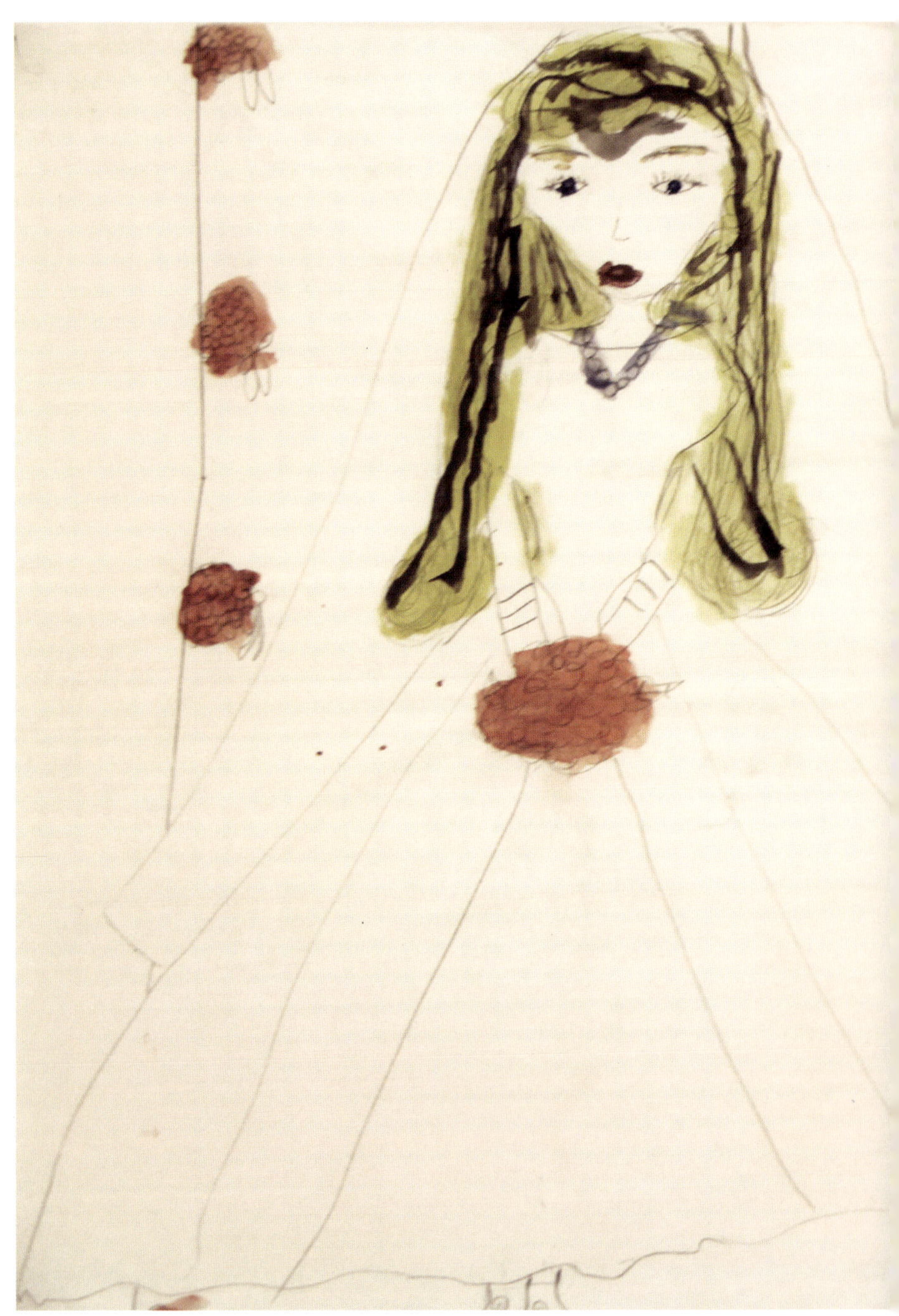

Unknown artist. Courtesy of the Permanent Collection of Children's Museum of the Arts

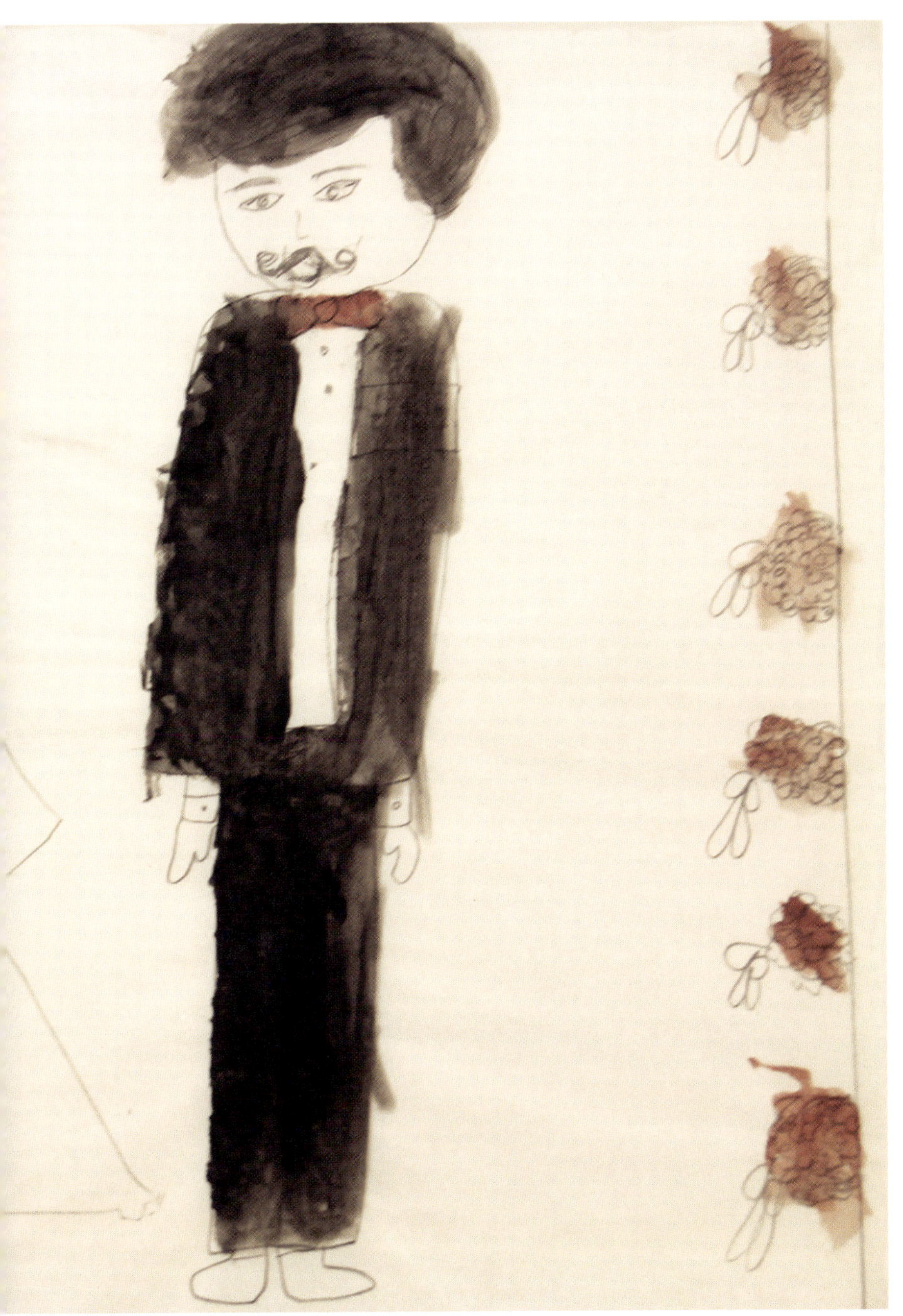

THE DOORS

The doors in my house
Are used every day
For closing rooms
And locking children away.

Brian Andrews, aged 10, Australia

With the time scribbled under our eye,
smudged by our explanations.

Now we are shadows of ourselves,
Engrossed in the magical
therapy of crap TV.

Where is the word for I don't wanna
face the streets,
so we call the days our own,
and make sleeping bags our graves.

Edie MIchael, aged 13, UK

MESSAGING

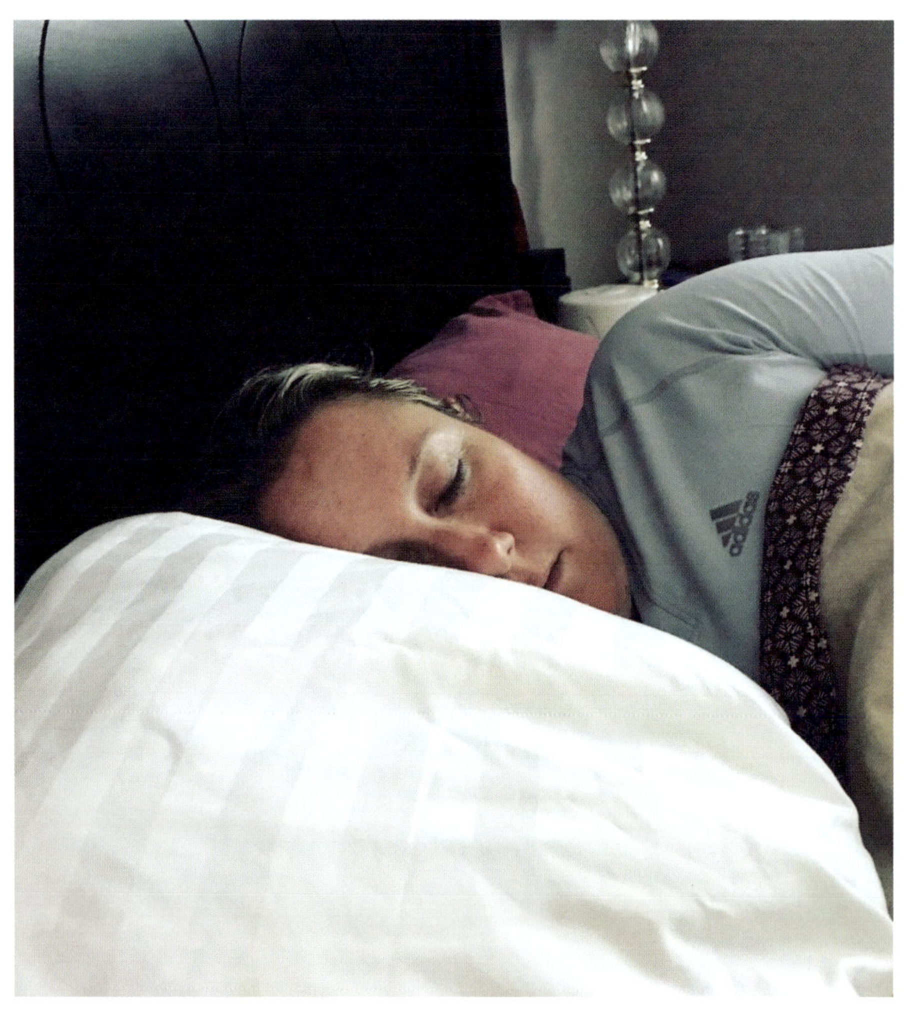

Photo by Vivienne Fricks, aged 3, USA

MOM,

I'm going to run away tomorrow at 9.30 when you and Dad are sleeping.

Be sure to say goodbye forever.

Emily

PS I will be packed tonight

Found: Emily's note. Details unknown

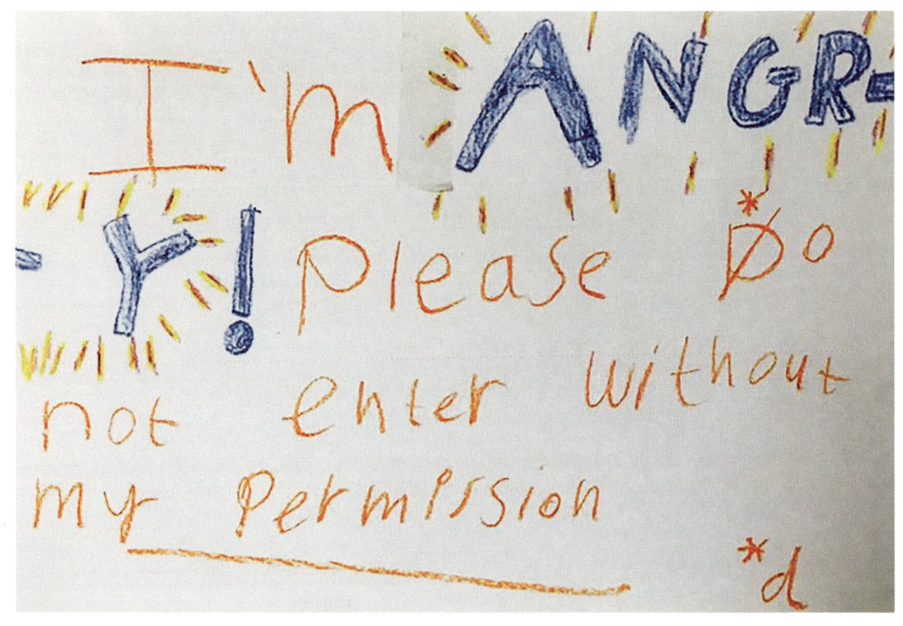

Verette Gatti, aged 6, UK. Tom Gatti (father), 'The holiday is going well.'

Emil Porter, aged 5, UK. Max Porter (father) 'Our third child, Emil, found out that as a baby he came on a book tour with me. It is a triumphant moment in his relationship with his older brothers. He made a poster for their wall.'

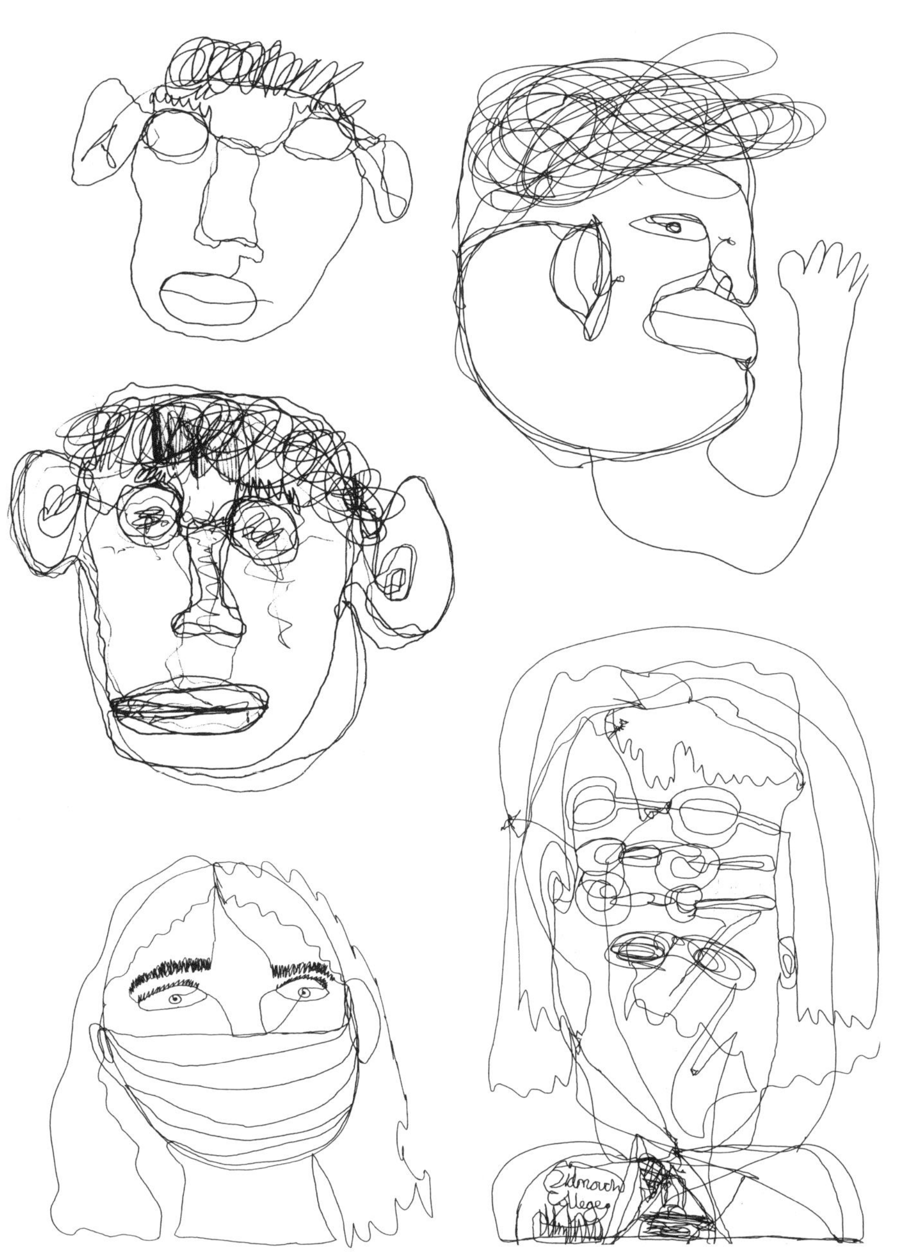

Drawings by children from Sidmouth College, UK, 2021

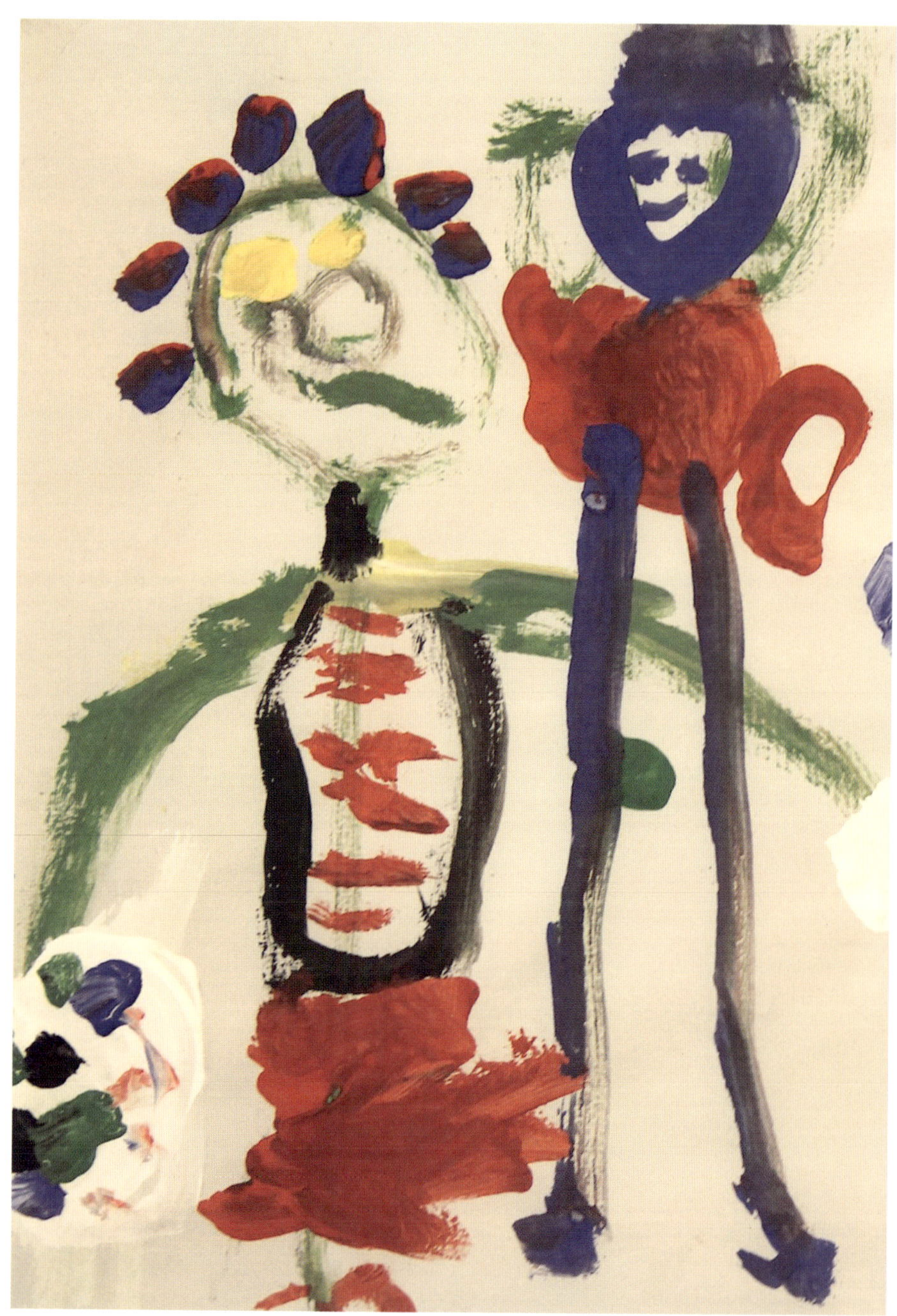

I'm Drawing (detail), Sharon Shang Chao, age unknown, USA. Courtesy of the Permanent Collection of Children's Museum of the Arts

Out of control letters in the wild

When I write my letters get out of control. Like when I am trying to draw an N and instead of an N I get an H instead of an N so I have to fight the H and by the time it's an N its five times bigger than it should be. Sometimes when I try to write in the lines the letters try to run away and escape out of the page and those letters sure are annoying.

Nuri Musa-Young, aged 7, UK

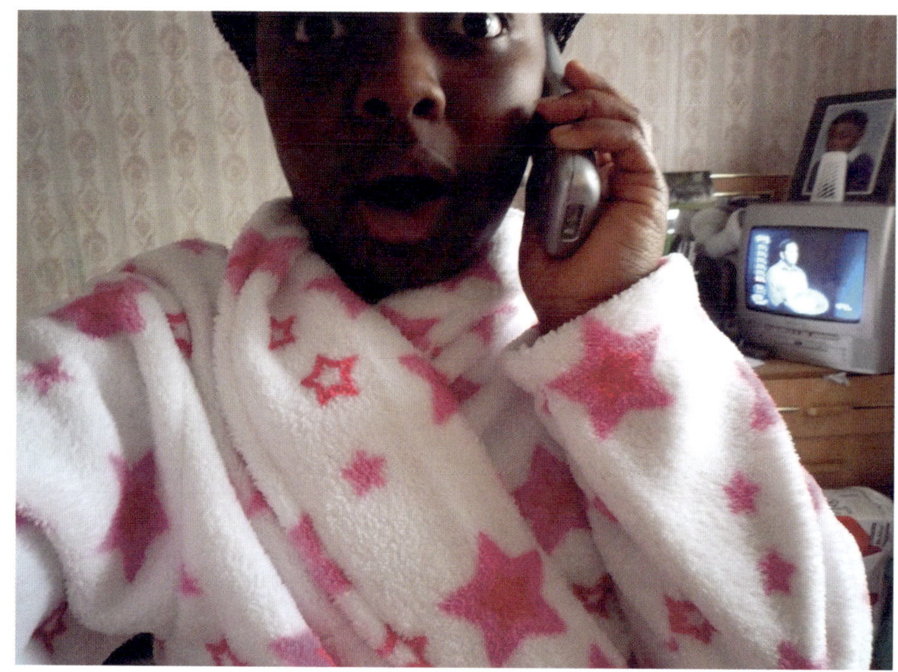

Photo by Sally, aged 10, UK. Courtesy Cubitt Artists

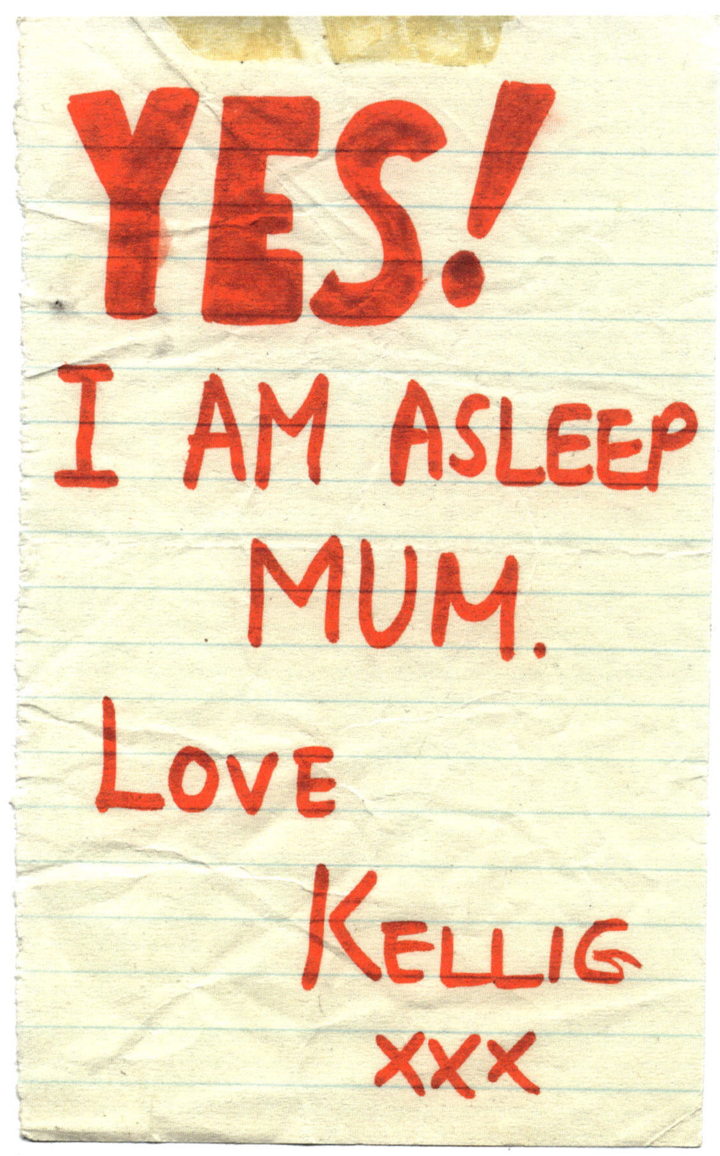

Found note, details unknown

MY DREAM?

There would not be any killing and war.
Also I dream that Justin Bieber would just go away.

Found note, details unknown

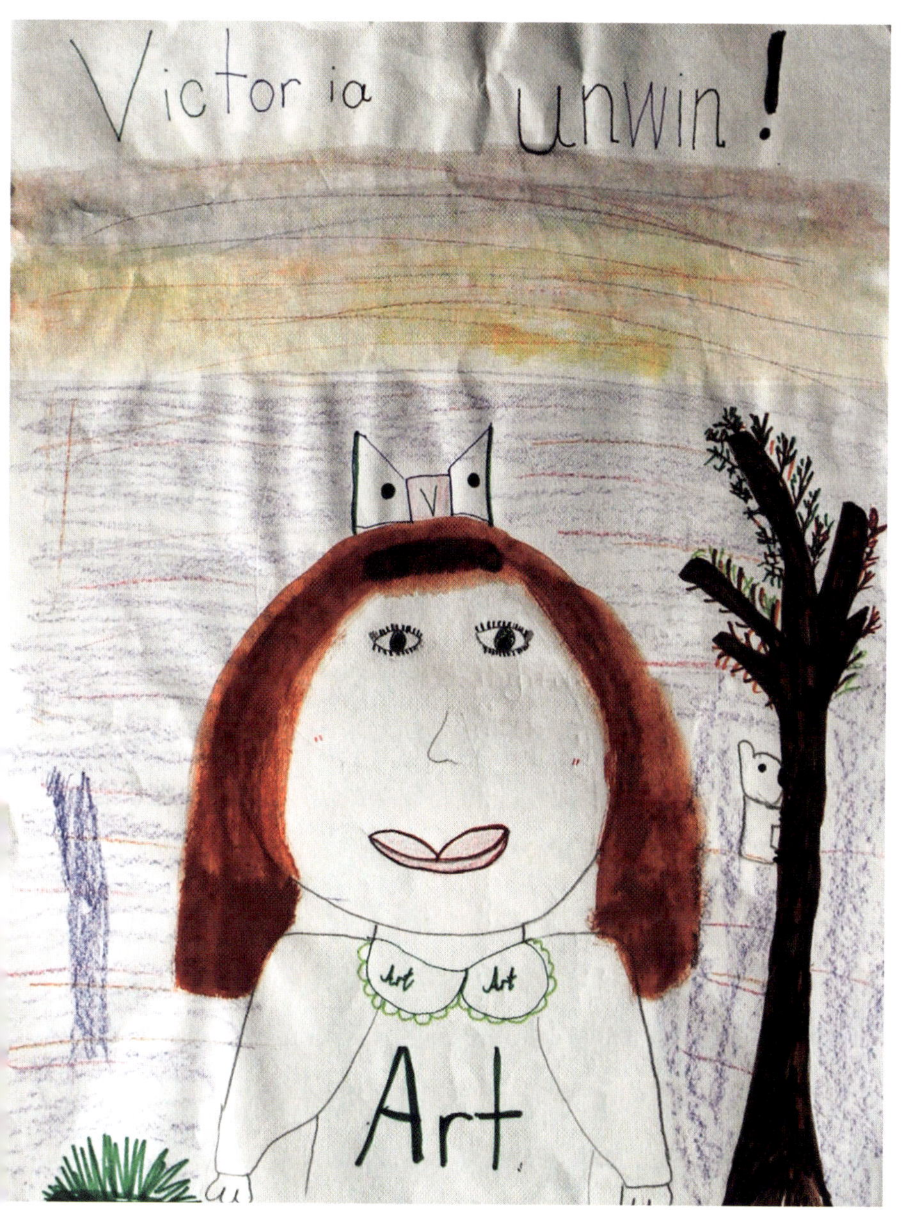

Victoria Unwin, my friend, Francesca Spence, aged 8, USA. Courtesy of the Permanent collection of the Children's Museum of the Arts

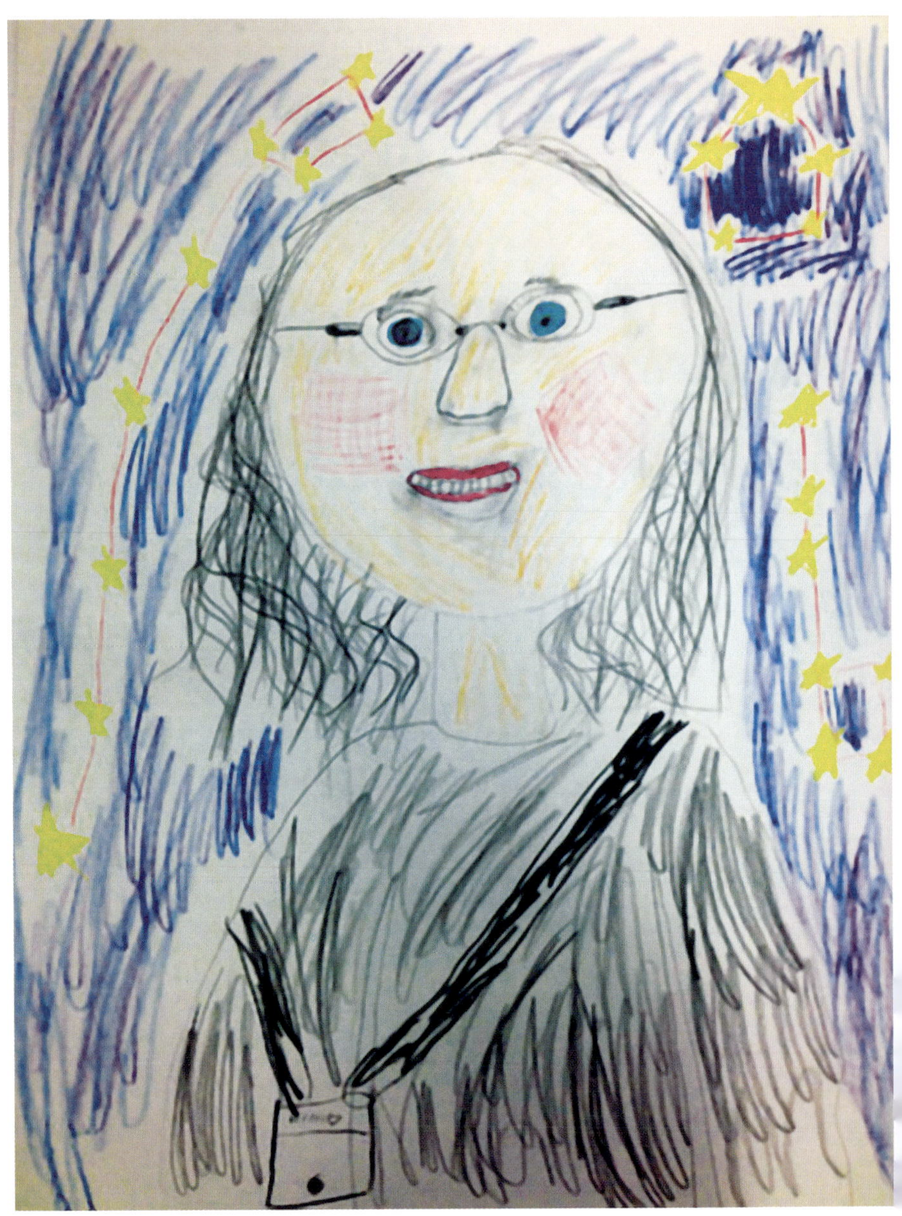

My Mom, Nella Craft, aged 7, USA. Courtesy of the Permanent Collection of Children's Museum of the Arts

Dear Mom and Dad dont
bother to give me dinner
im not that hungry

~~Love~~ From
The saddest
person in the
world

Found note, details unknown

DEAR GOD

Thank you for the baby brother but what I prayed for was a puppy.

Joyce

Found note, details unknown

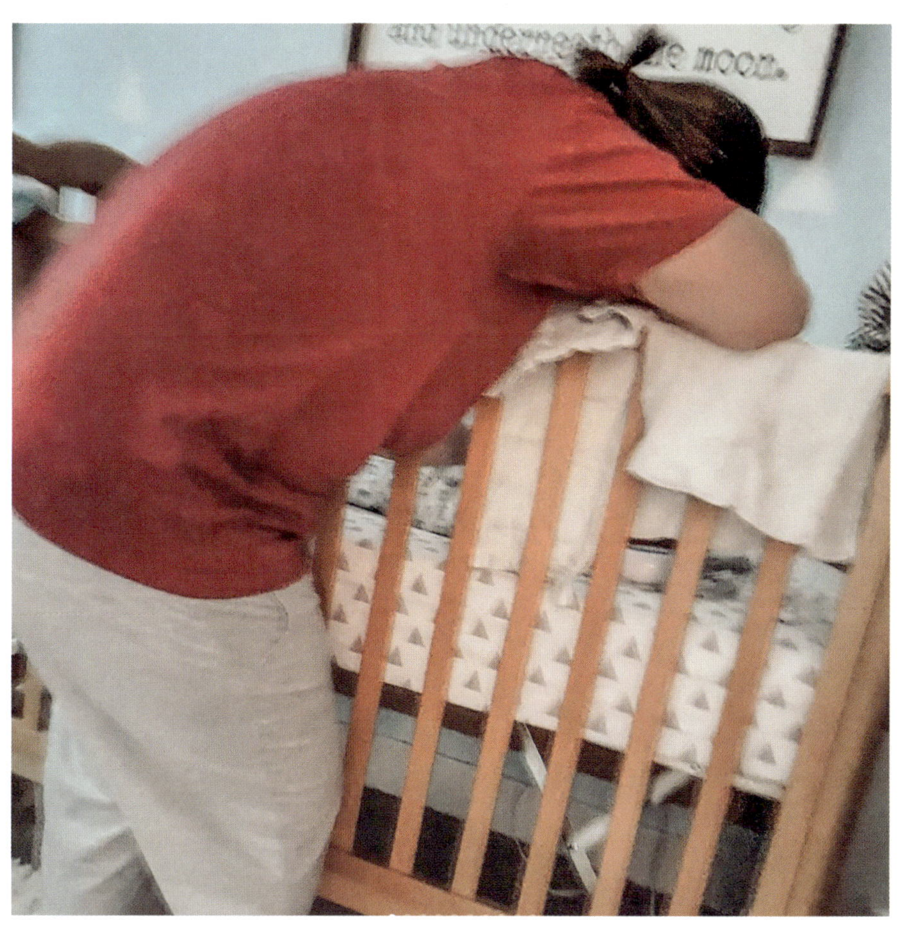

Exhausted mother, photo by Nate, aged 4, USA

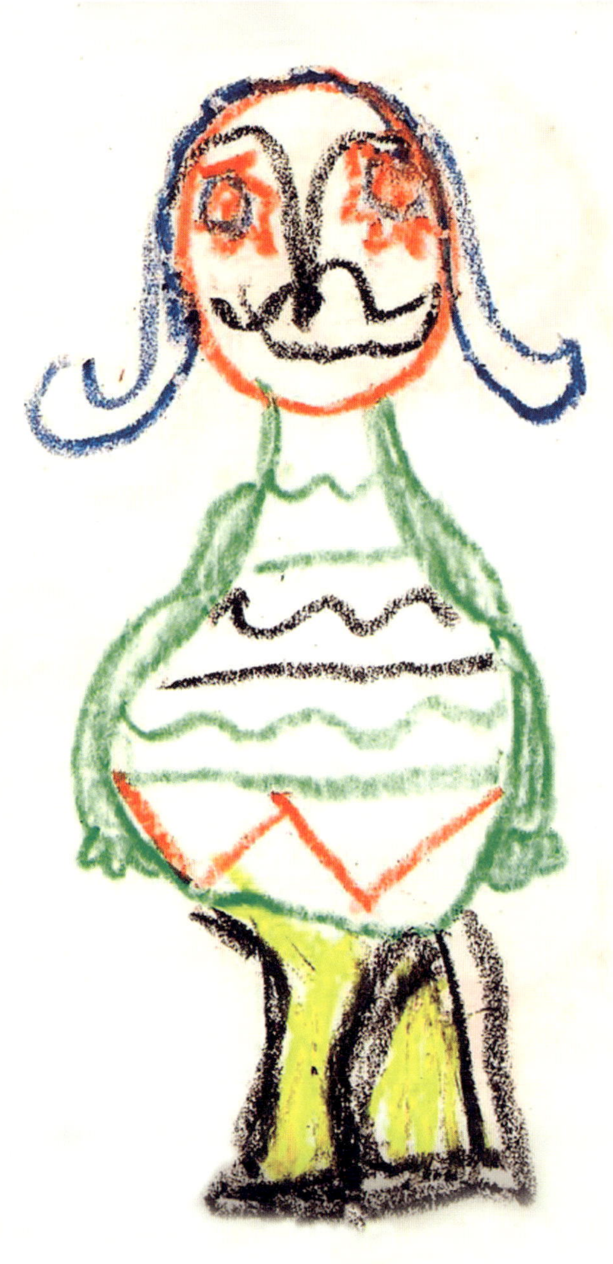

Found drawing, details unknown

When I grow up
I want to get a hat
and put it on.

3-year old's answer to the question *What do you want to be when you grow up?*

ROOM by Keir Peters

This spectacular piece of art raises the question

What is Messy?
What is Tidy?

It is truly astonishing and a wonder of art.

'Just checked in on 8-year-old who's supposed to be tidying his bedroom. He's reading a book,
 surrounded by Lego and silently pointed to this note on his wall. I give up.'

I am good

I am good | I am good

I am good | I am g

I am | I am g

I am good | I am good

i am good | I am good

I am good | I am good

Jessica Collins, aged 6, UK

Name ___________________

Name the quadrilateral.

Rectangle   Rhombus   Parallelogram   Square

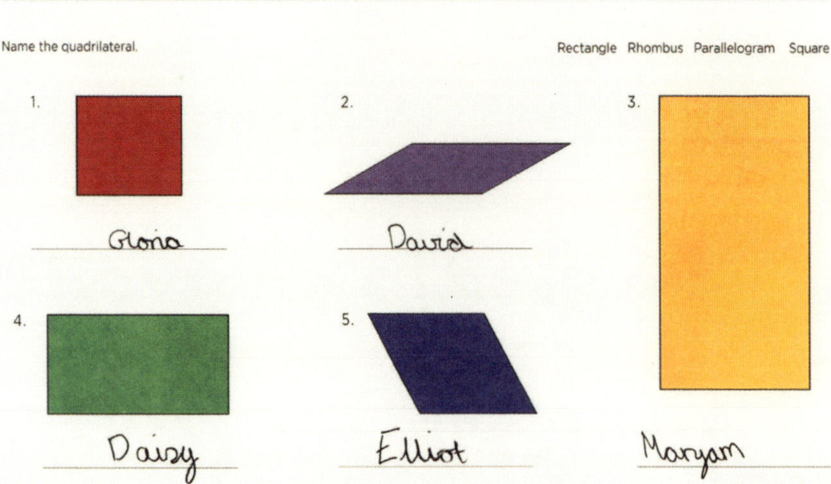

Find X

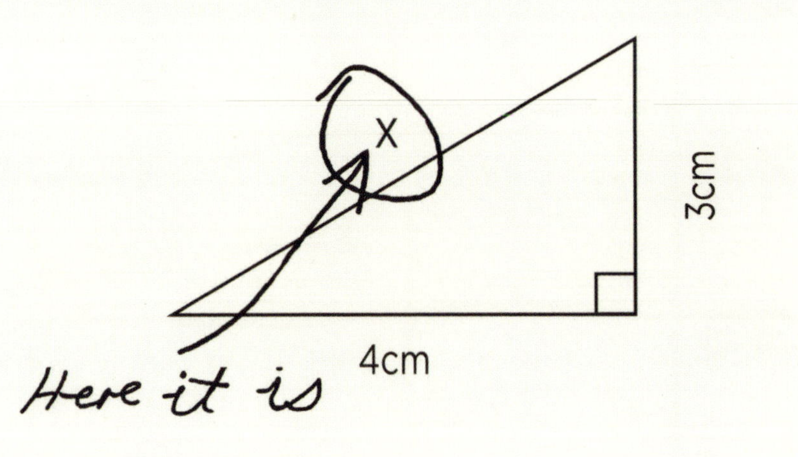

Found maths homework, details unknown

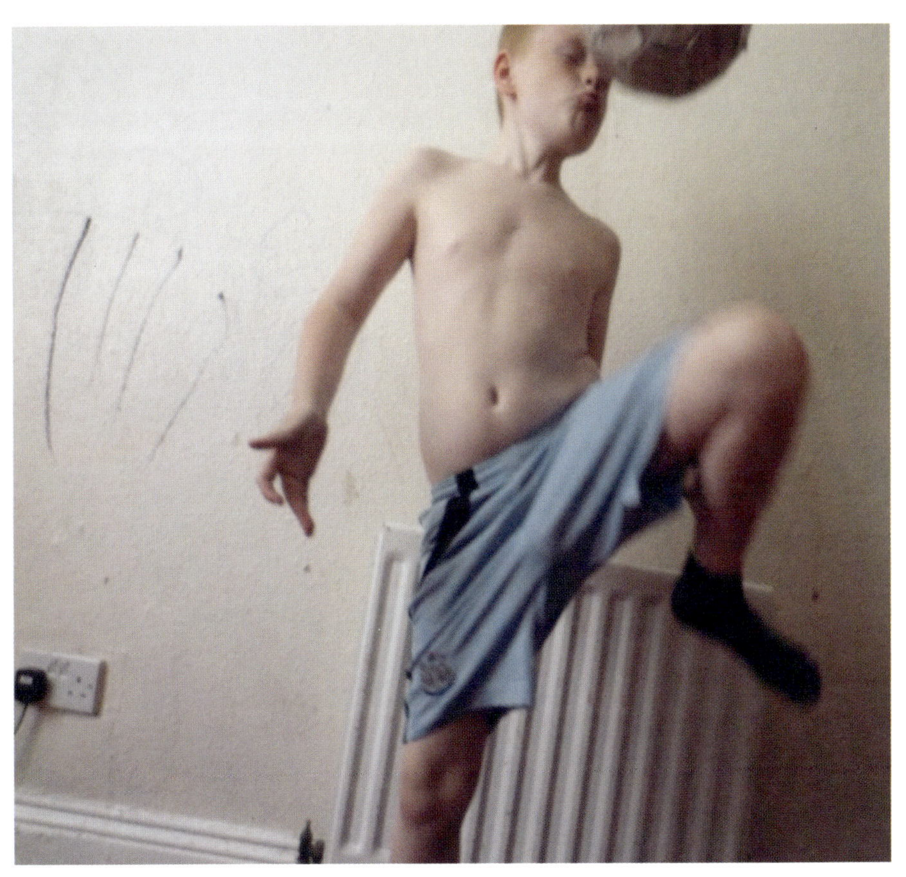

Photo by Sarah, aged 8, UK. Courtesy Cubitt Artists

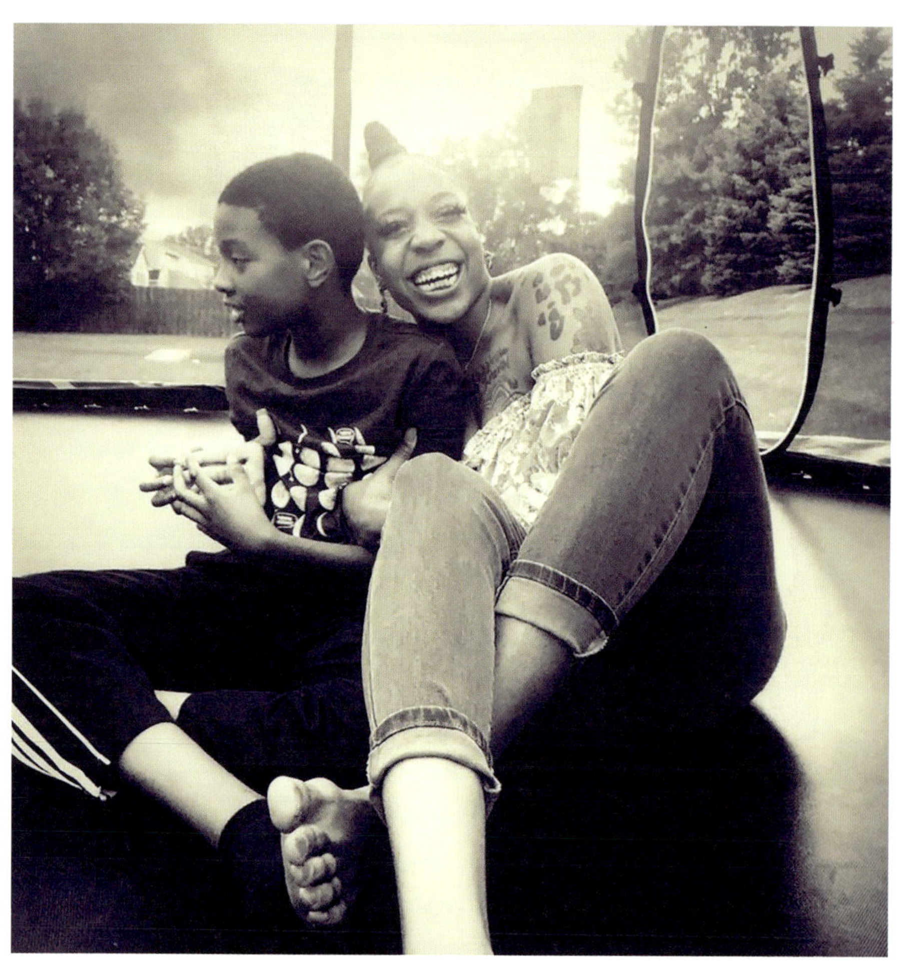

Unknown photographer, aged 3, USA

TODAY WAS MY FIRST ART CLASS.

This is what my teacher looks like.

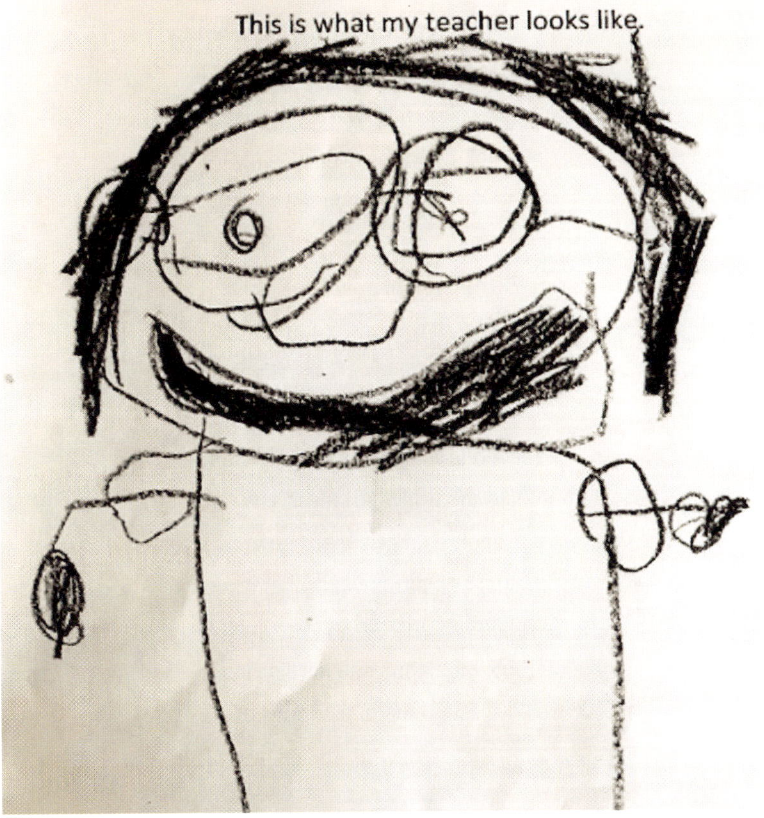

Found drawing, unknown artist

Never put nature aside for telivision.

You burned my feelings today and

I am warning you never to do what you

did today again.

Found note, details unknown

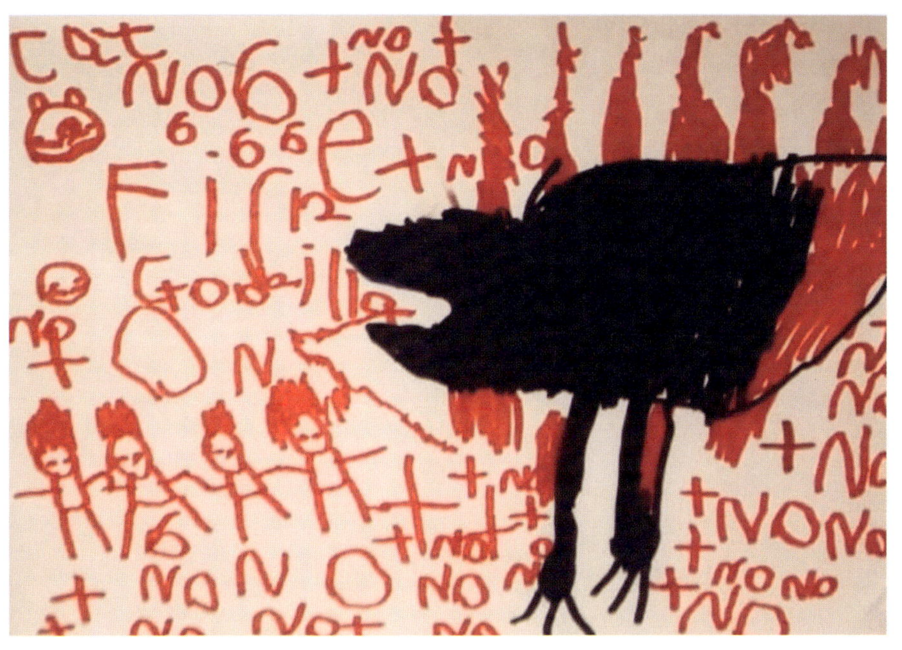

Godzilla, Ruben Gluba, aged 5, UK

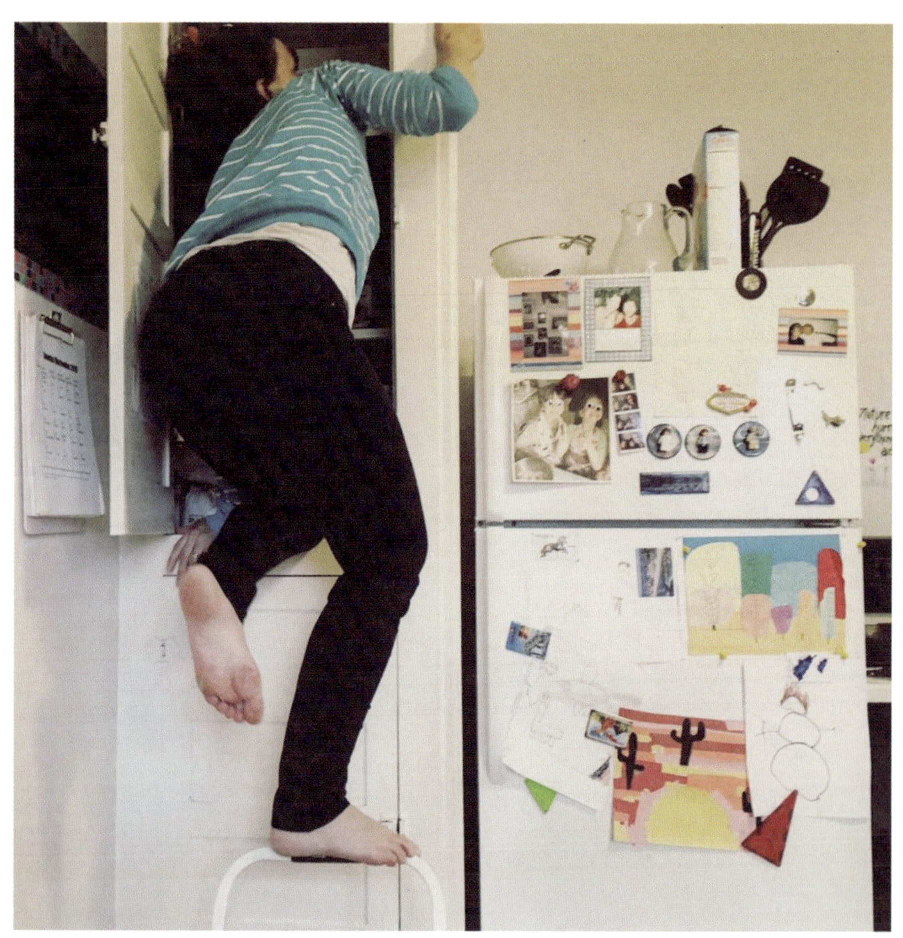

Photo by Eleanor, aged 8, USA

FLOW OF EVENING

Free play
Play with my bear
Make a list
Take a bath
Sarah comes
Hang out
Eat supper
Go to bed

Found: schedule of a girl aged 5

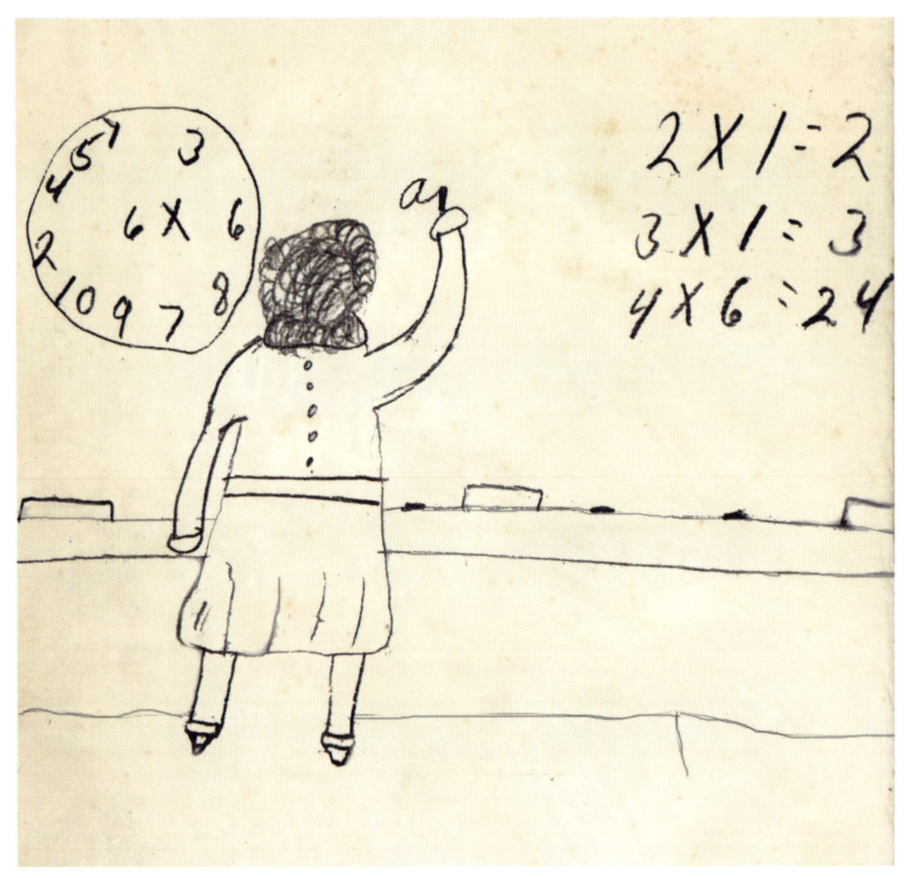

Found drawing, details unknown. Courtesy Steve Feldman

I like Mrs Edwards. She is my techer.

I like it when she does meth with us.

Found note. Details unknown

PLAYING

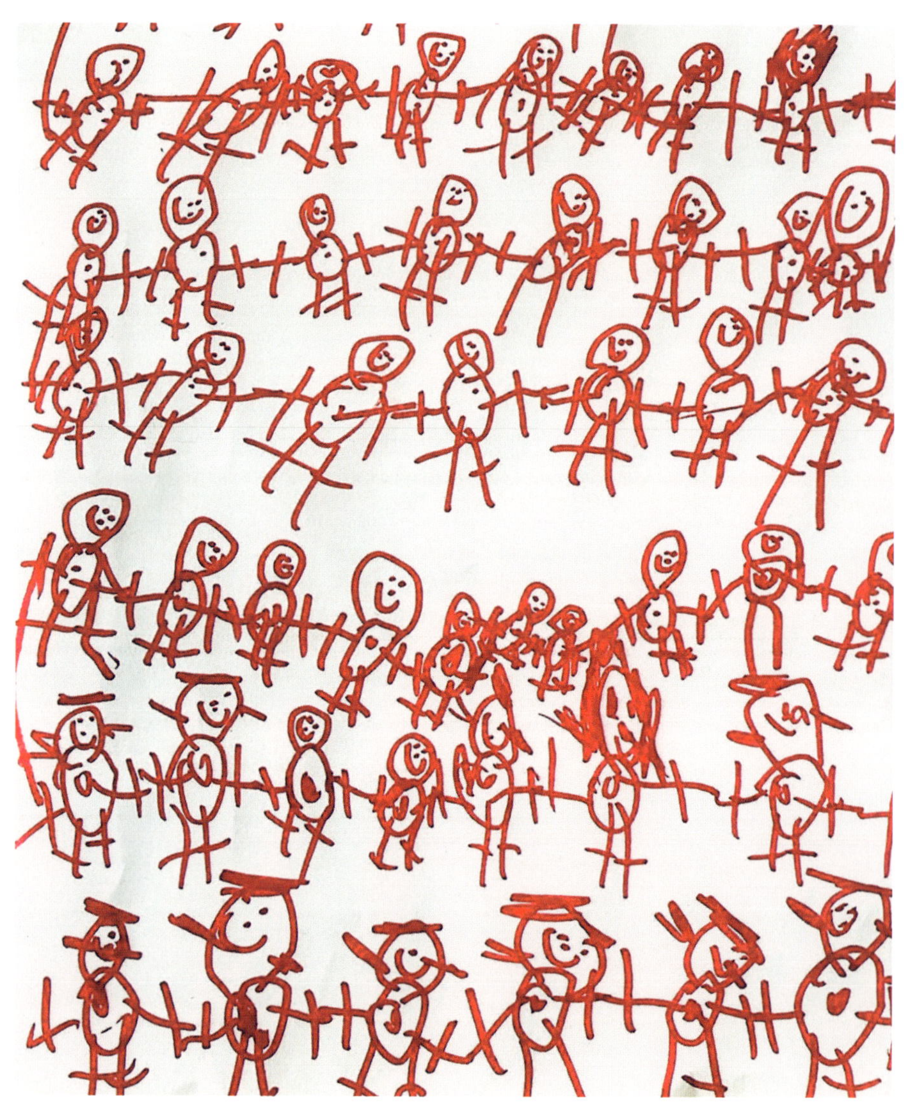

Granny, A.J., aged 4, USA

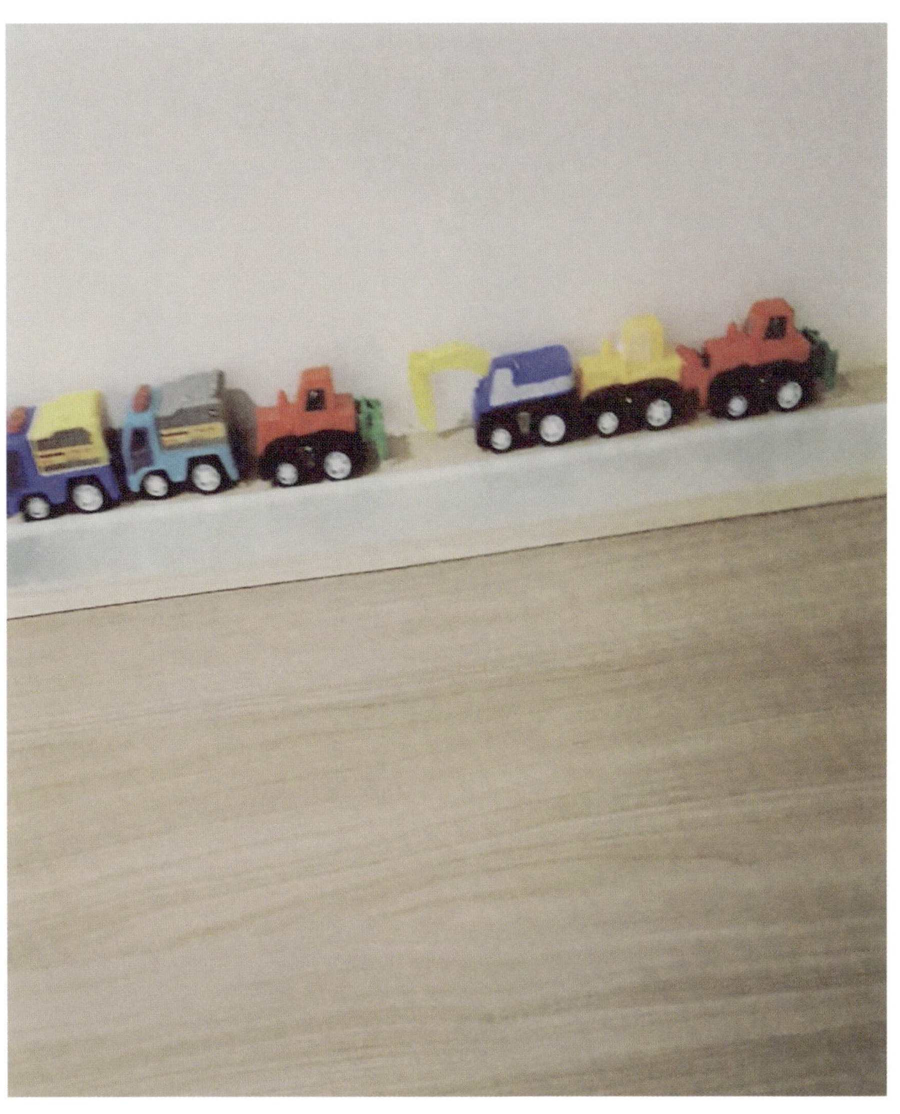

Photo by Iani Ian, aged 3, USA

SAM'S FOOTBALL GAME

Old, tall and fat, and blue eyes as blue as the sky. That's how Sam looks. He is kind, funny, brave, and he loves football. He is also a cow. Sam is playing football. It is a stormy day at the stadium in New York. Sam's football team is winning. There are bears, crocodiles, tigers, lions, and elephants in the crowd The score is nine to three.

Sam M., aged 7, USA. Courtesy Valencia 826

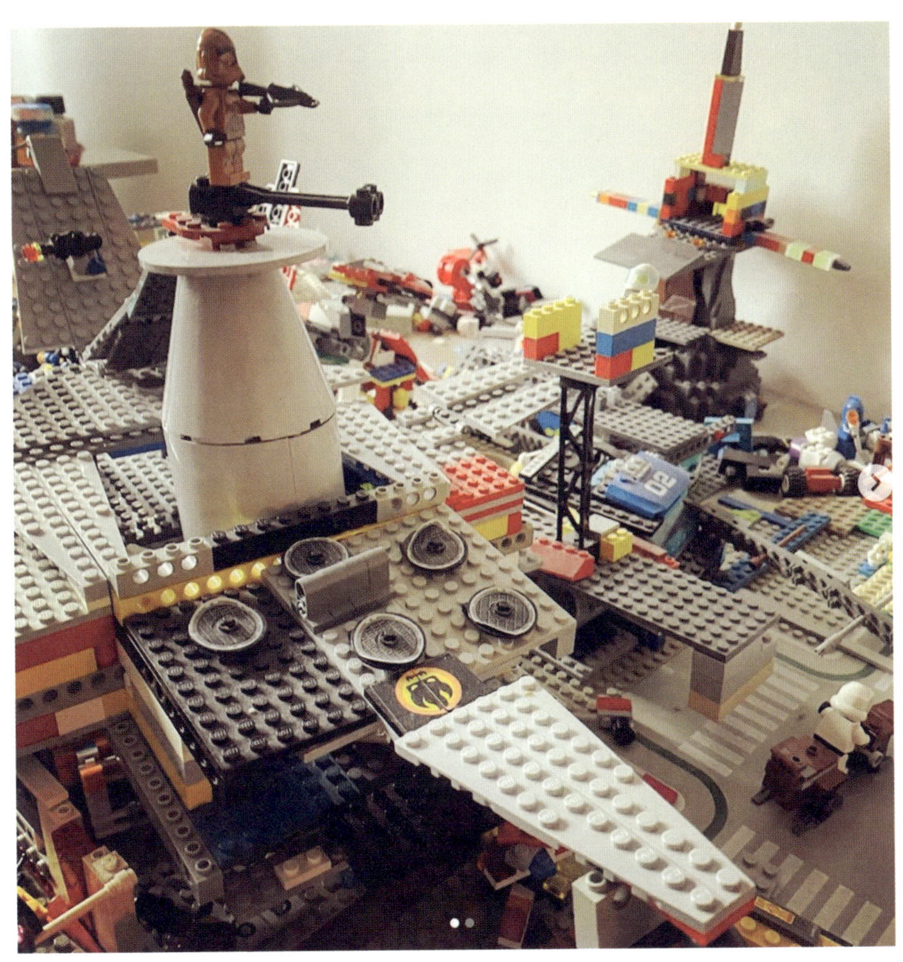

Unknown photographer, aged 8, Poland

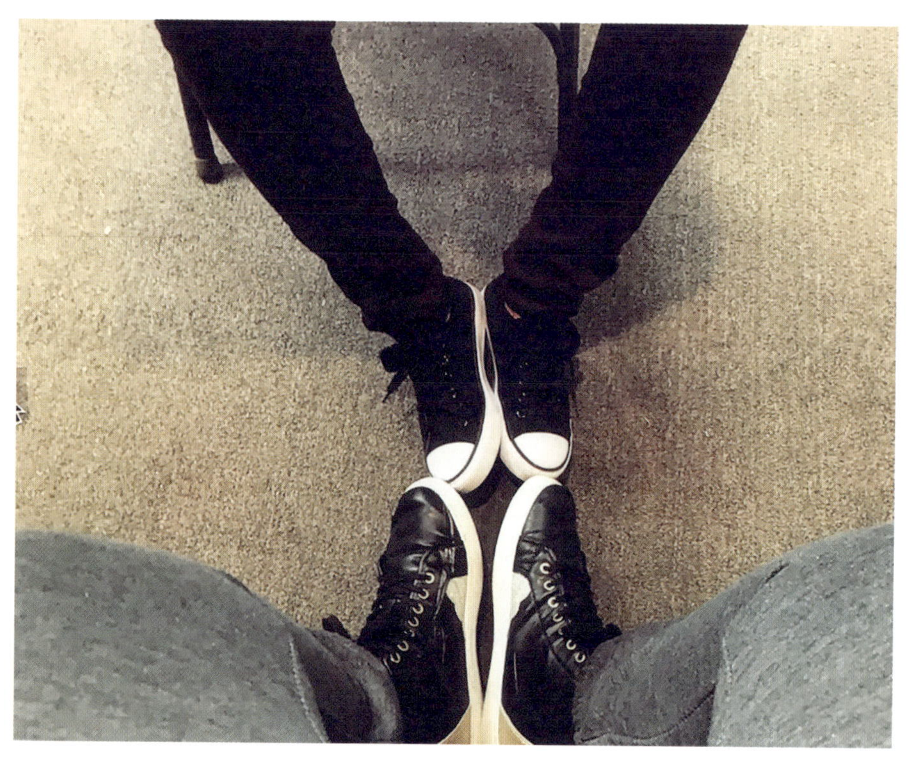

Unknown photographer, aged 9, USA. Courtesy Through the Eyes of Children

THE FALL

Shoe

Shoe lace

Shoe lace race

Trip, fall

Chase

Hugo Morganti, aged 10, New Zealand,
Courtesy Poetry Box

MIRROR! MIRROR!

As I look into the mirror I see my face,
Then I talk to myself.
Then I play like I am in jail.
I pretend that I am bad.
I pretend sometimes that I am on a stage.
I sing to myself. I introduce people.

Deborah Ensign, aged 7, USA

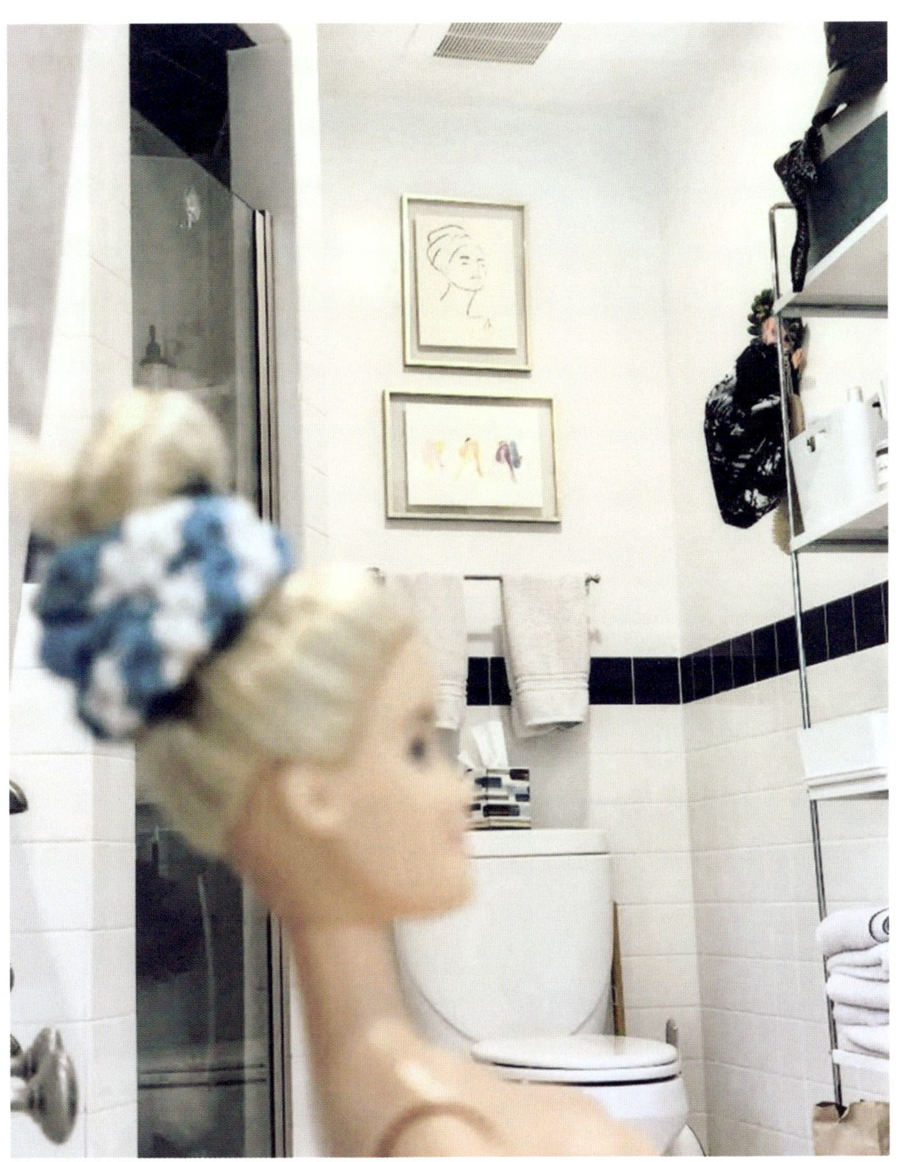

Unknown photographer, aged 3, USA

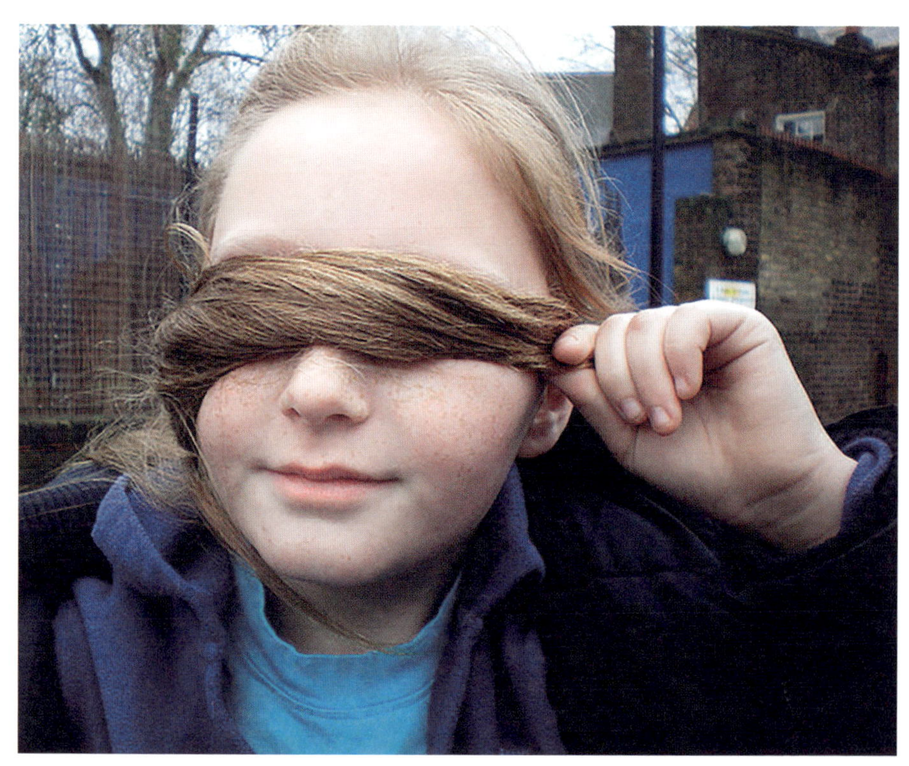

Unknown photographer, aged 8, UK. Courtesy Cubitt Artists

FLY'S NEW DINER

Welcome to Fly's New Diner
Come in, come in
Here is our menu
Feel free to order
If you can be heard above the din

Menu
Cheese and shrew sandwich
Roasted branch with honey fried eel
Scorpion tails and roasted quails
Rat meat sausages
Caramelized snails
Toads' eggs and turtle brains
Boiled tarantula with hemlock sauce
Ants' legs, bat's teeth burger
Mice innards on noodles
Meerkat's paw in frog's eye soup
Nightshade and fishbone pie
Elephant ear and duck's foot gloop
Fly Agaric mushrooms with lentils

Lettuce fries and curdled carrots
Nettles, broccoli and cabbage on noodles
For the vegetarians among you
Purple hyacinth cake
Caramel cheesecake with snakeskin flakes
Marshmallows afloat in curdled milk
Raspberry avocado cream
Guacamole jam
Starshine and sun's essence
Melted eye of lamb
Aloe vera and spider spit tea
Seaweed sauce
Essence of flea

Come in come in
Would you like to taste?
'Sorry, sir. I'm late today'

Do come back another time
'No thank you, sir.
I'll stay away'

Sarah-Kate Simons, aged 13, New Zealand. Courtesy Poetry Box

On friday night we go to the pictures

My mother says be back for nine o'clock

I say look well if the pictures arnt finished.

Still be back.

I think to myself she do not understand.

Anne, aged 13, UK

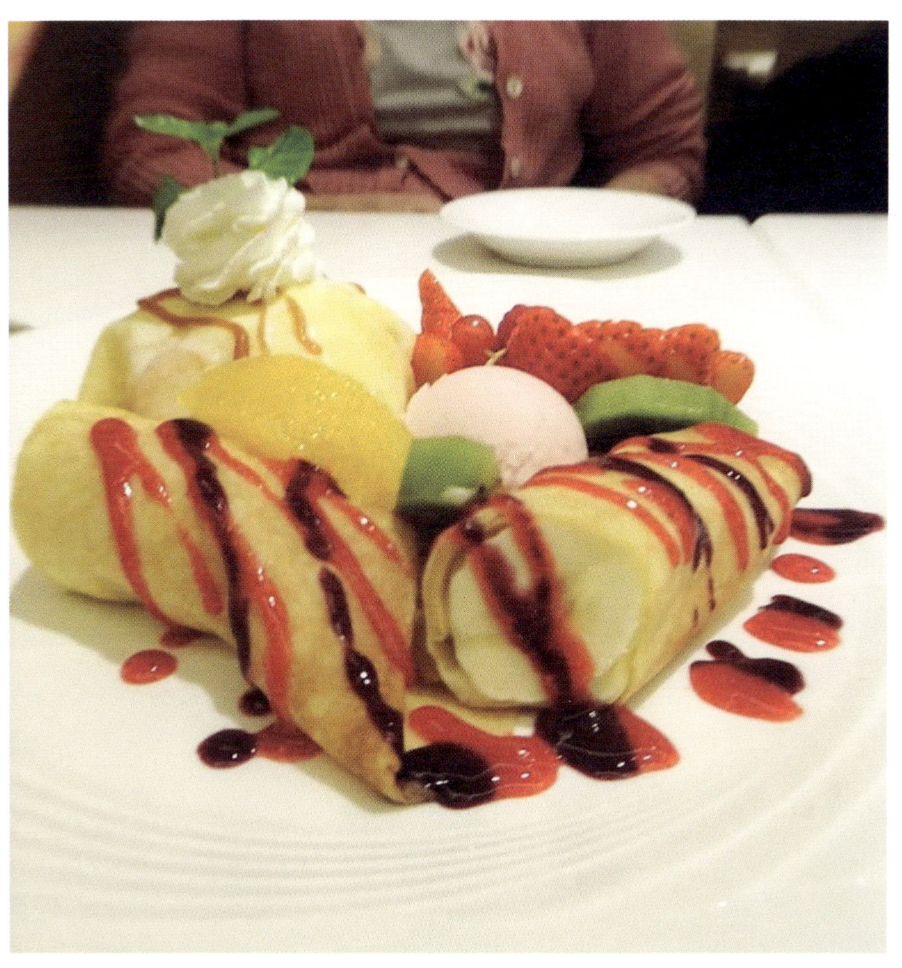

Crêpe, unknown photographer, aged 6, Japan

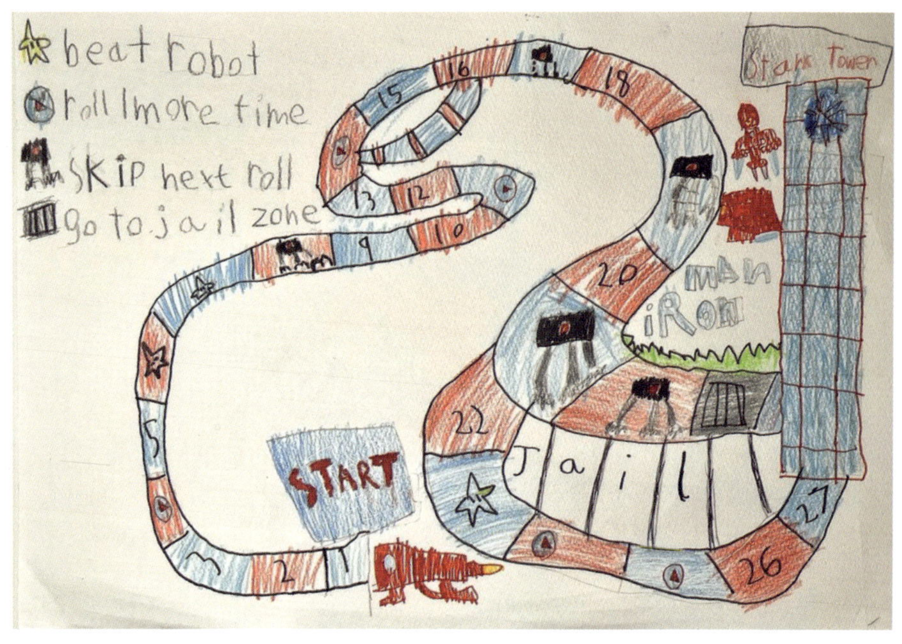

Iron Man Dice Board Game, Aidan, aged 5, Japan

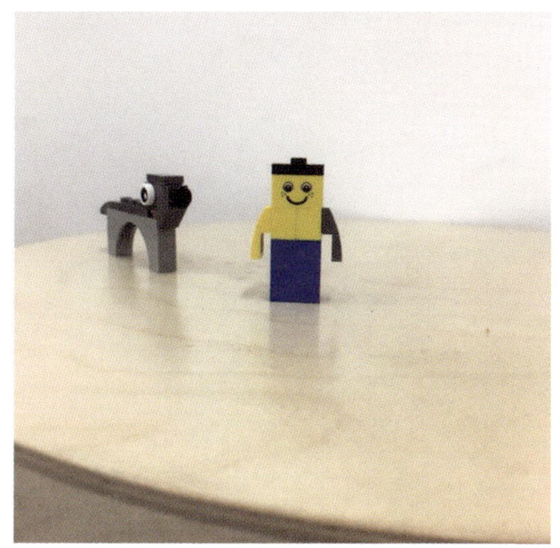
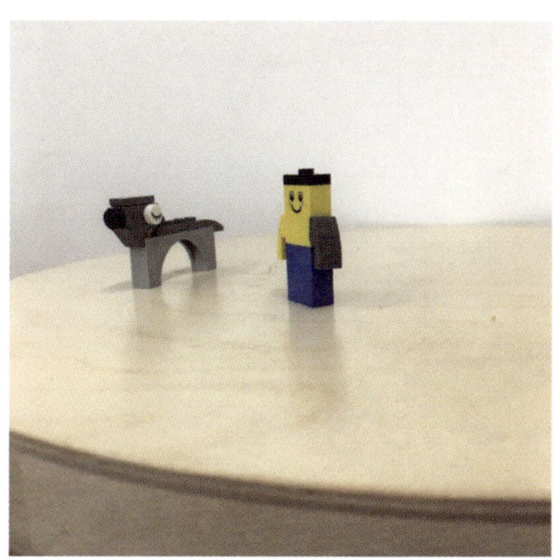
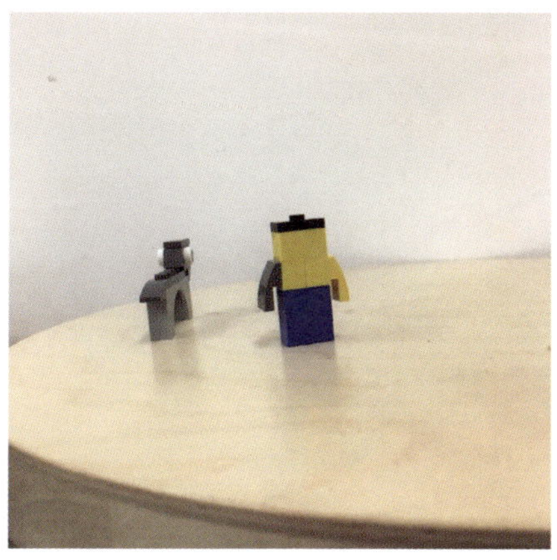
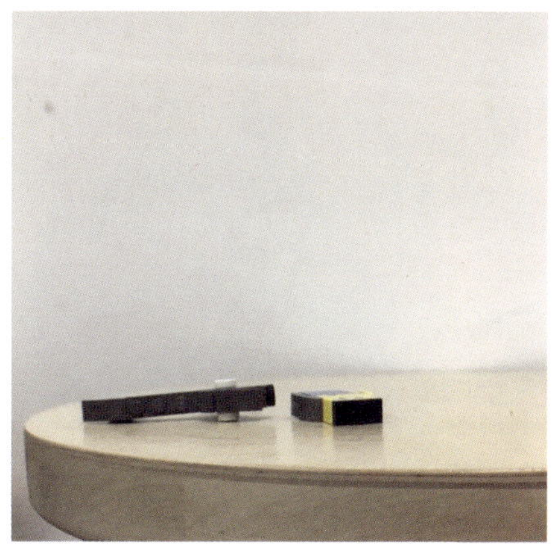

Unknown photographer, aged 5, Japan

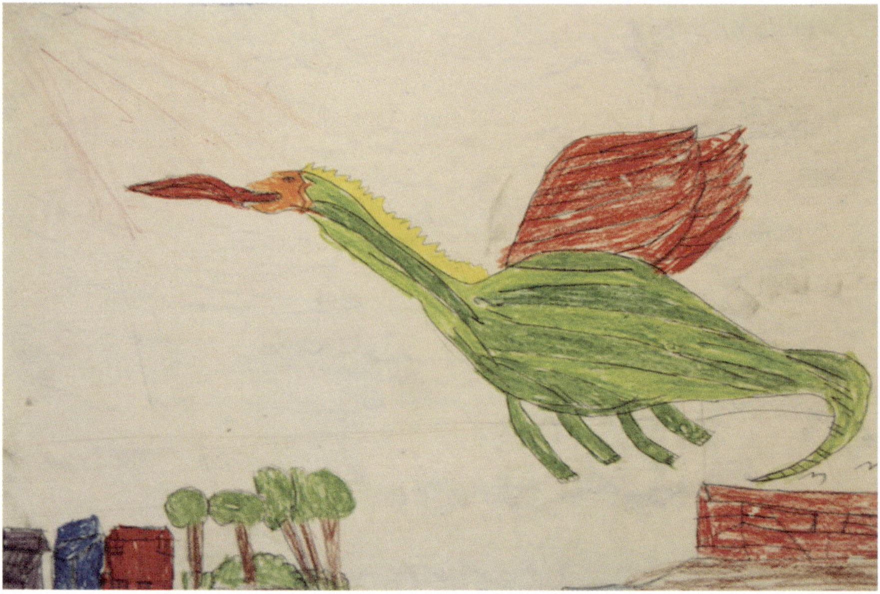

Dragon, Salam Al Hajeri, aged 10, UAE. Courtesy of the Permanent Collection of Children's Museum of the Arts

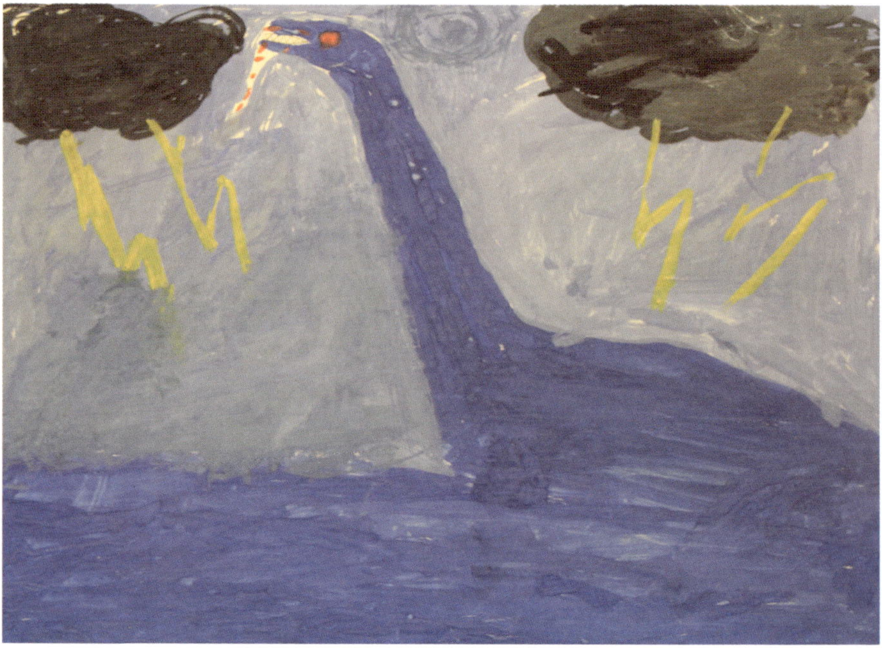

Arif Roiz, aged 11, Syria. Courtesy of the Permanent Collection of Children's Museum of the Arts

THE COLLECTOR

I am a collector.
Not just stamps and stickers,
Books and Barbies,
Bits of glittery rock.
In my mind I store all sorts of things:
Whispers from the playground,
Games we'll play at lunch time,
The pattern of the pavement,
Reflections from the mirror.
Other pictures stay locked in me:
The faces of the hungry,
The ruins of bombed houses,
Dirty, crowded hospitals,
There way they chop down forests.
I don't choose to collect these things.
They just jump into my mind.

Ellen Coffey, aged 7, UK

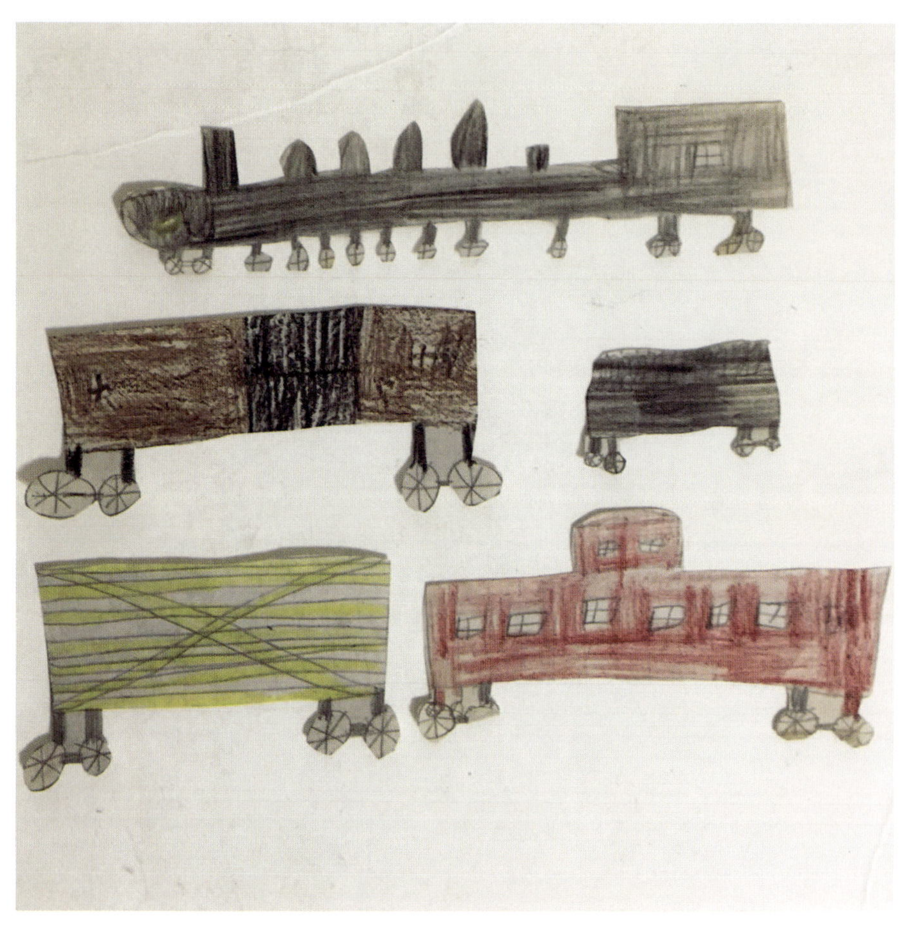

Unkown artist, USA. Courtesy Steve Feldman

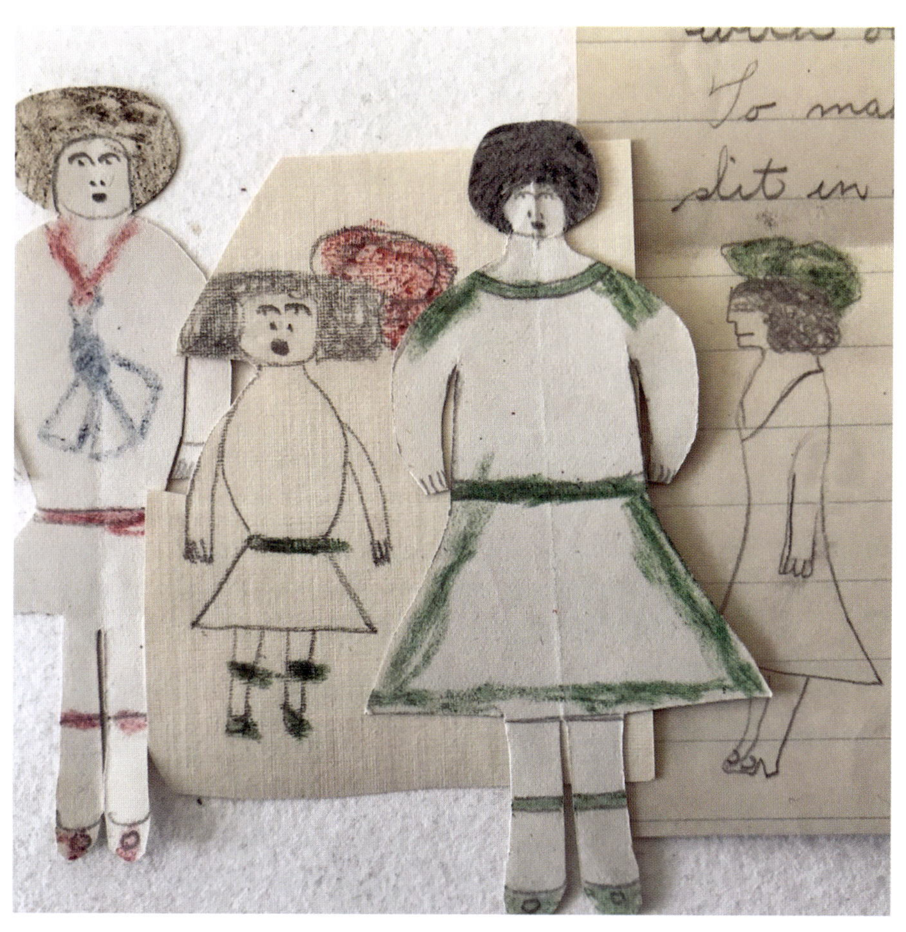

Unknown artist, USA. Courtesy Steve Feldman

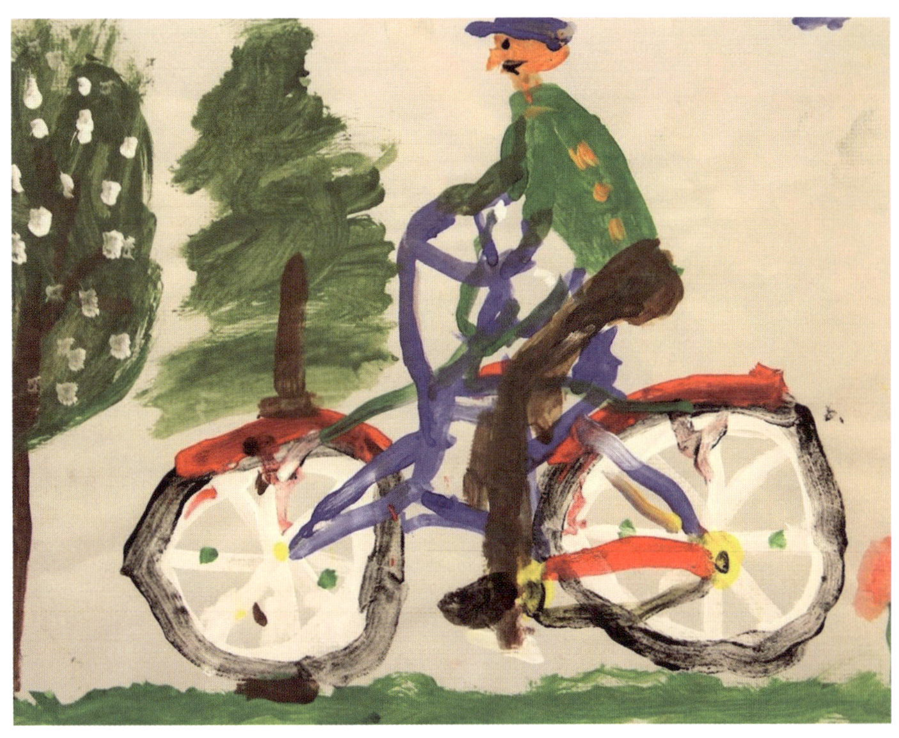

Bike Riding, Benjamin Kon, aged 11, USA. Courtesy of the Permanent Collection of Children's Museum of the Arts

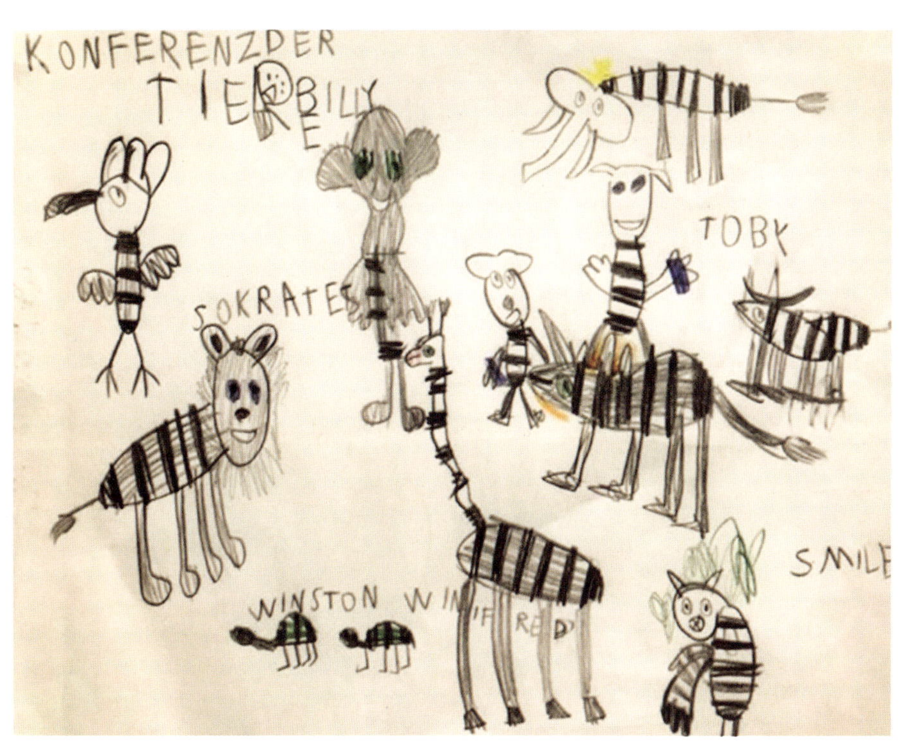

Conference of Animals, Lenni, aged 6, Germany

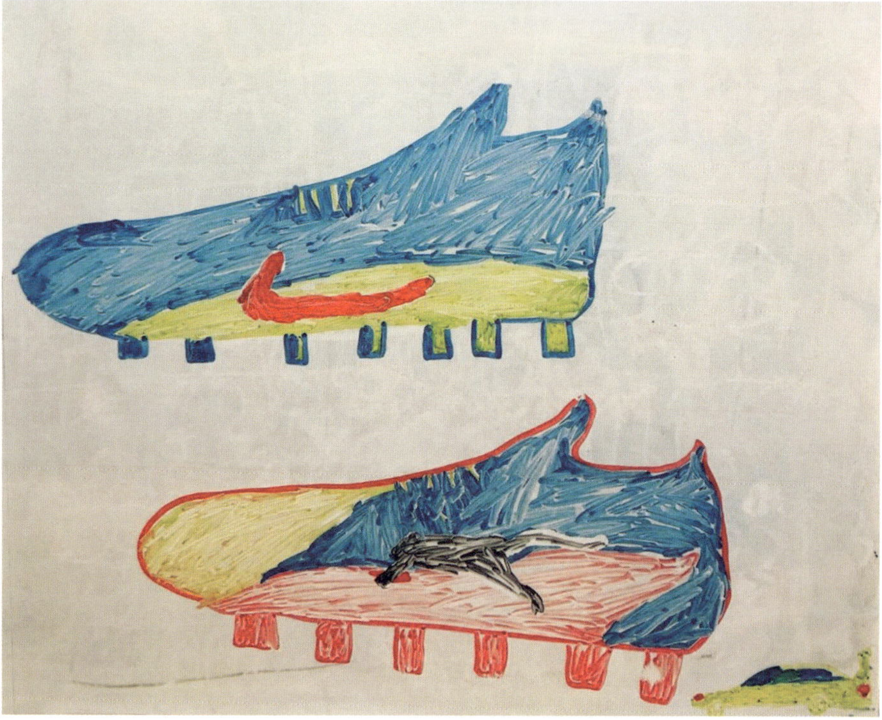

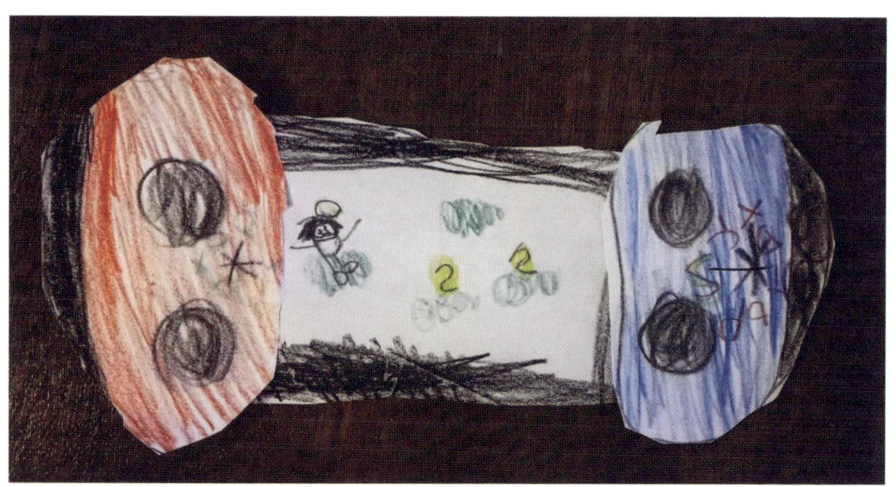

Nike or Puma, Keremin Sarilar, aged 7, Turkey

Nintendo Switch, Dide Balozdemir, age unknown, Turkey

I HAD A DREAM

I had a dream that I was a movie star, a pop singer. My band was called
WHO OWNS MY LIFE, my name was Tobias and my surname was Strindberg.
I was playing who owns my life. When suddenly the tune went wrong and
everyone was throwing food at me, so I ran out of the stage and got another
job that was publishing in faber and faber. I worked on the top floor. I enjoyed
it there, when suddenly I made a lot of spelling mistakes in a book I had
published, so I got fired. I noticed I weren't good at anything so I became a
footballer but I weren't so good so I retired and got a wife. We had children
and I had a much happier lifetime.

Tobias Strindberg, aged 7, UK

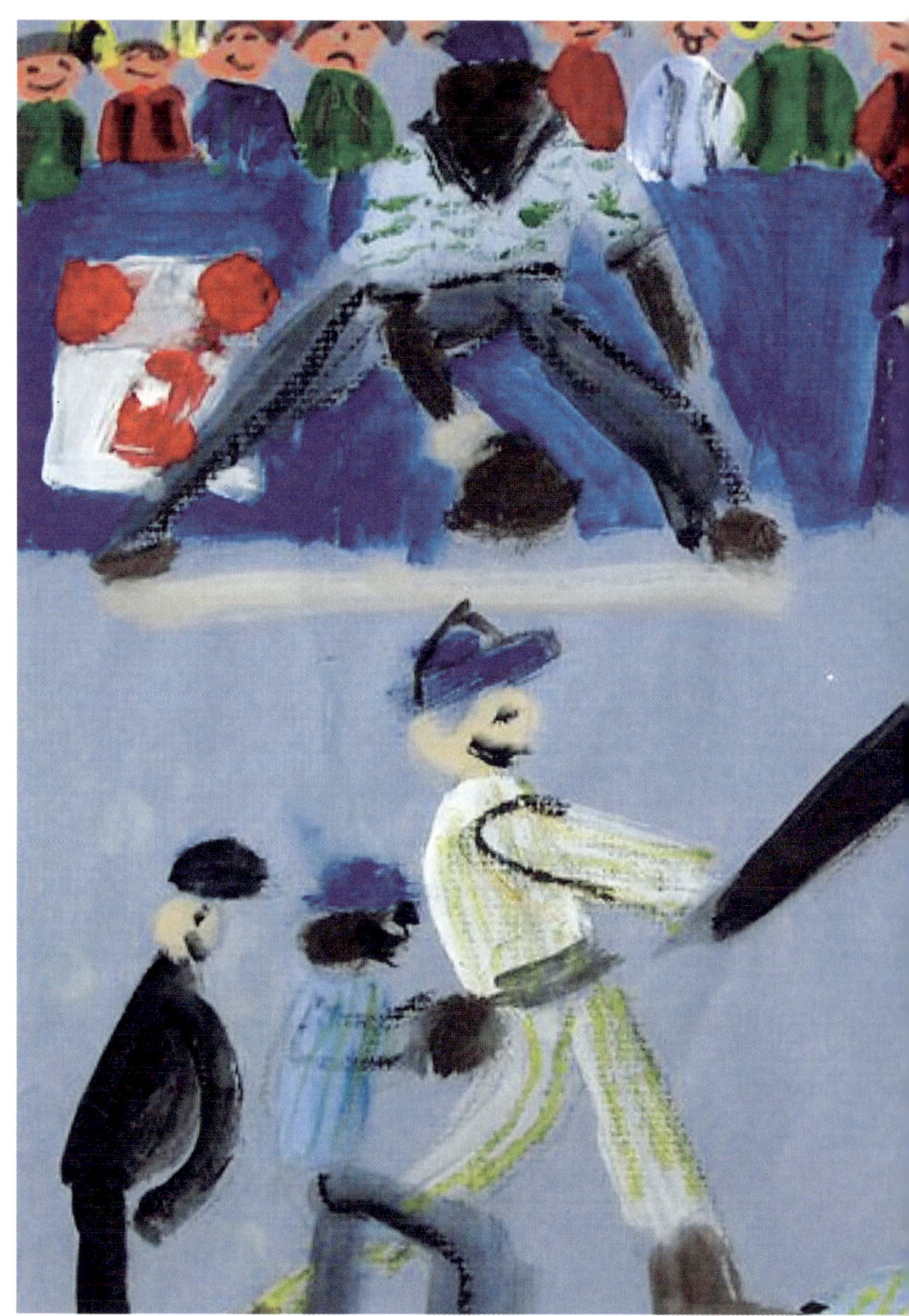

The Baseball Game, David Liu, aged 10, USA. Courtesy of the Permanent Collection of Children's Museum of the Arts

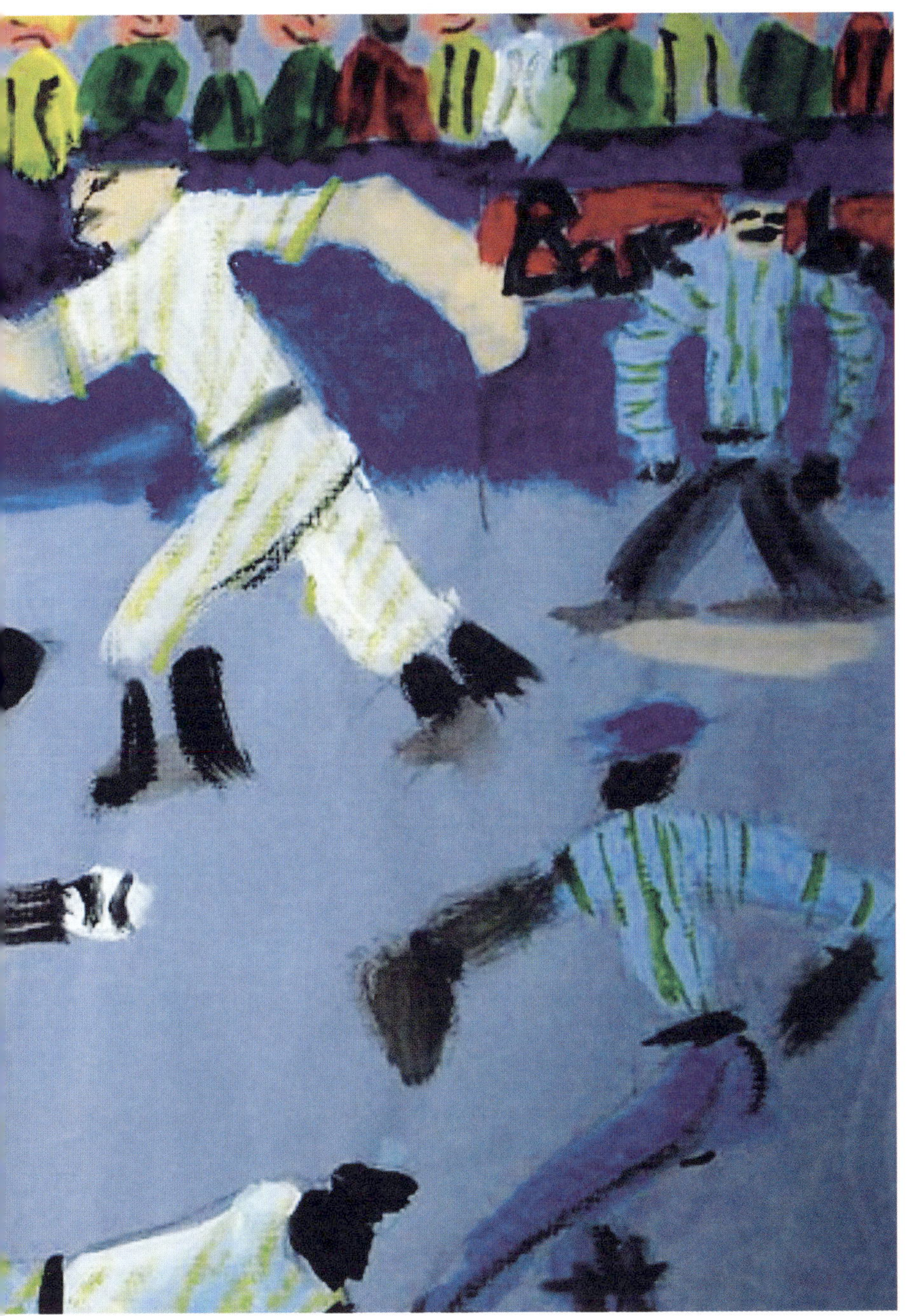

GAME OF DENTISTS

The night before I went to the dentist, my sister and I were playing at dentists. She stamped on the floor that made the chair go up. She then switched on a lite. She used a pair of pliars out of my tool set for pinchers. She used my bobble hat for the gas mask. She used a puddin dish for the thing that you spit your blud into. She used a poker for the drill and a glass of water for the mouth wash. She tied me to the chair with some thick string and tied a hanky round my neck. She got a lolly stick and prest my tong back to see which tooth to pull out. She put a bit of rock in my mouth to keep it open and put my bobble hat on me. She took it off and got the pair of pliars and pretended to pull out my tooth. She took a look at it and then gave me the water and I pretended to wash out my mouth. She untied the hanky, but she didn't untie me from the chair. She hit me about ten times and then ran off. I shouted mum to come and untie me. After that next time we play shes defenetly going to be the patient.

Simon Mark Abbey, aged 8, UK

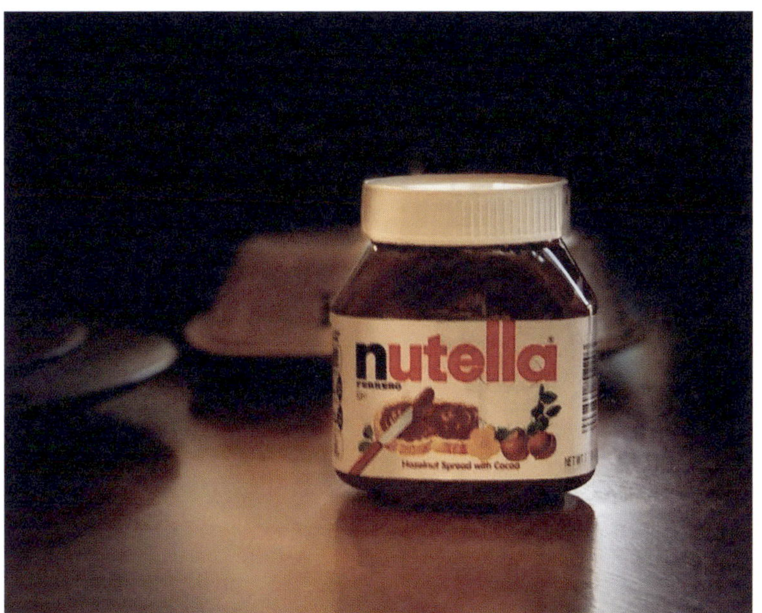

Found photograph, details unknown

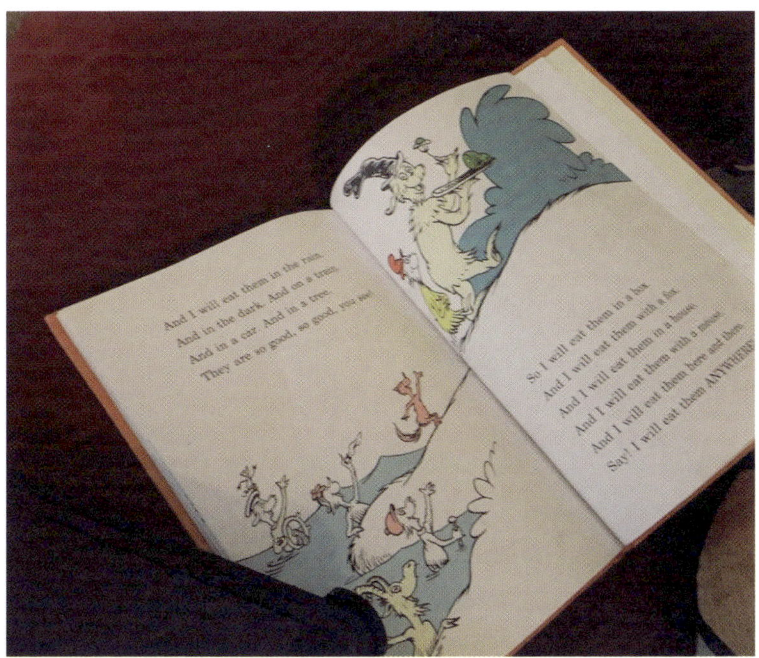

Found photograph, details unknown

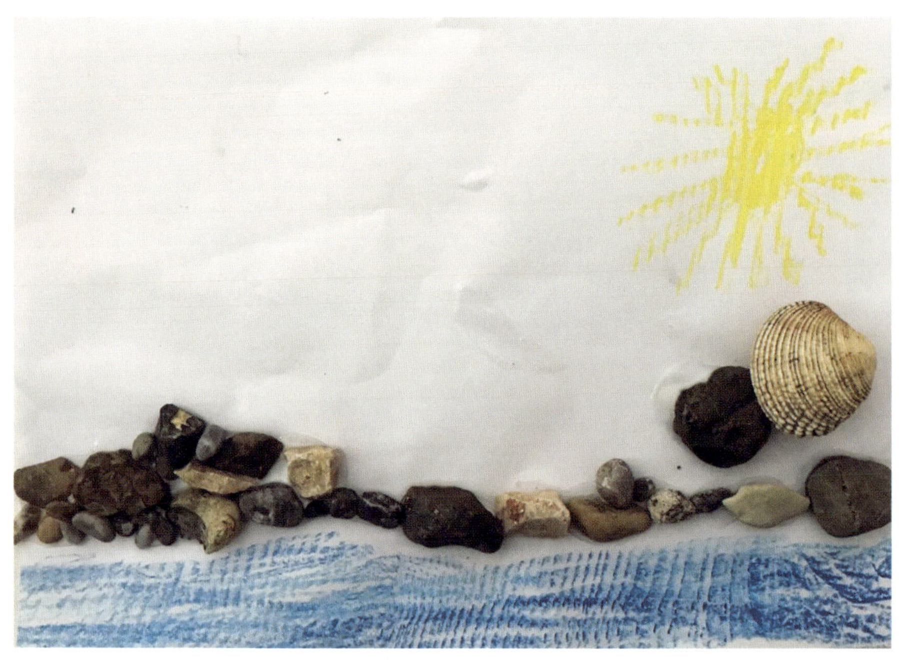

Unknown artist, aged 7, Turkey

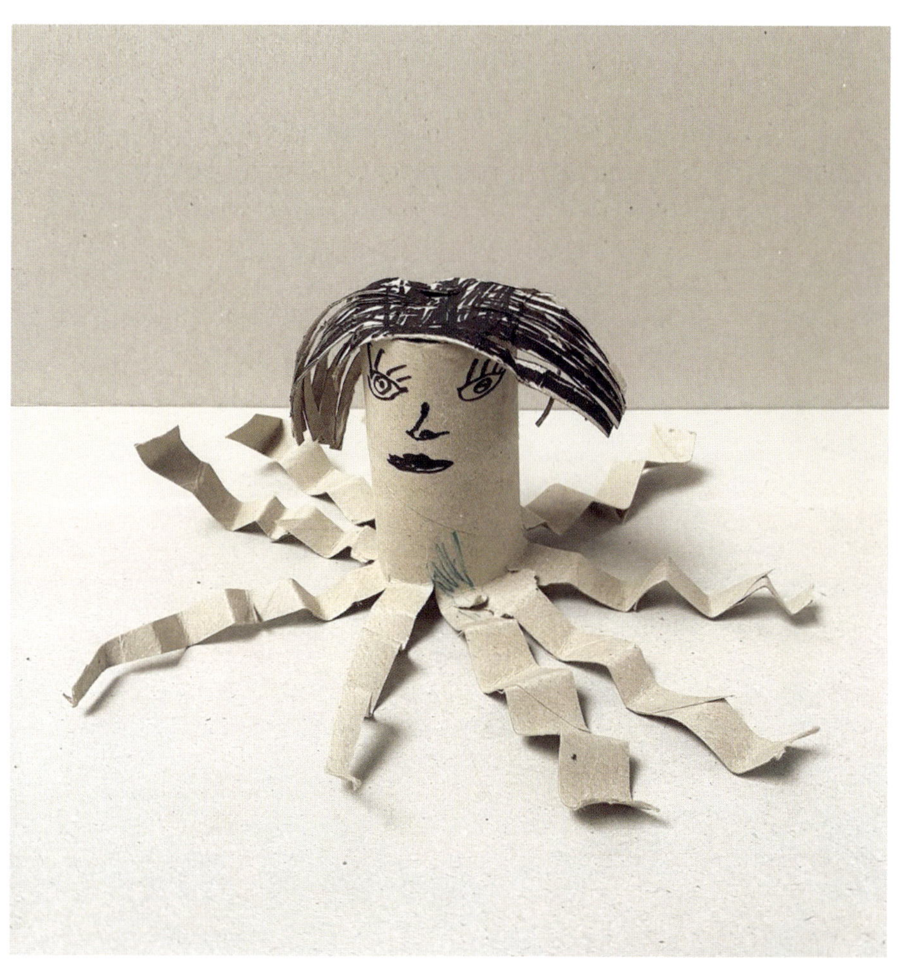

Tekla, aged 7, UK

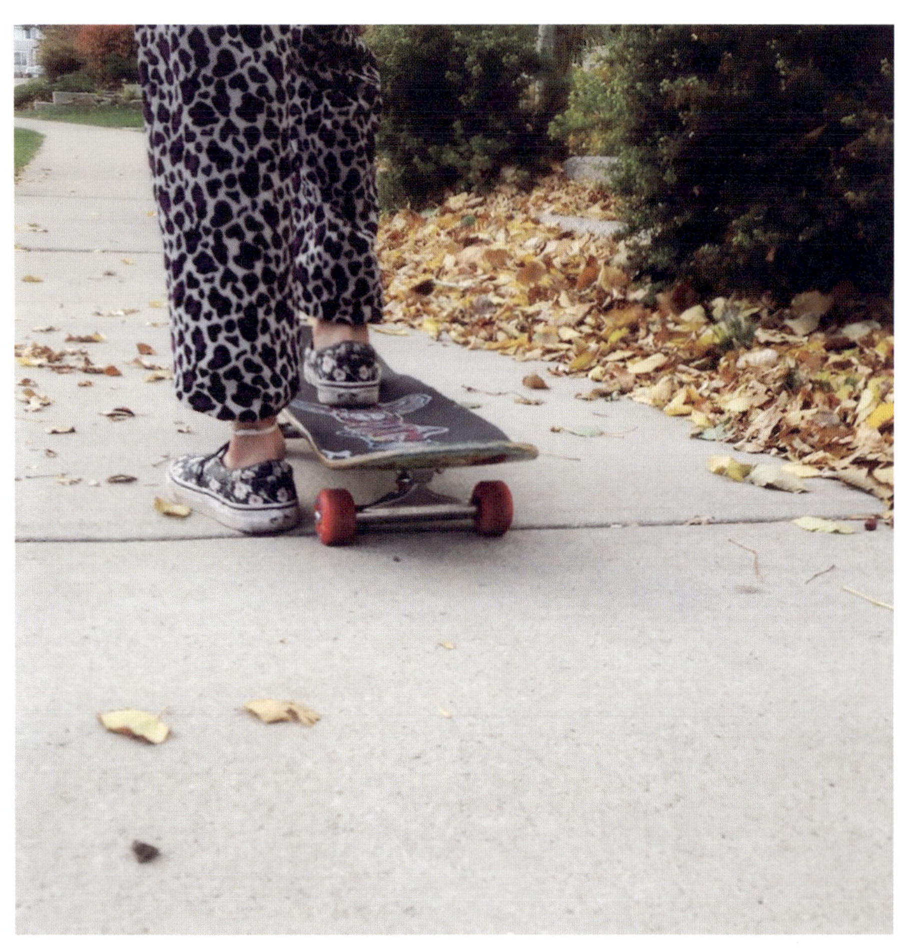

Unknown photographer, aged 10, USA

My perfect day would be to play with my doll for an hour then go outside for 2 hours have lunch have an ice pole play some more watch a movie go for a walk maybe play tag then hide and seek climb trees go in forest part of upton park come home have dinner have dessert go to bed.

Found note, UK

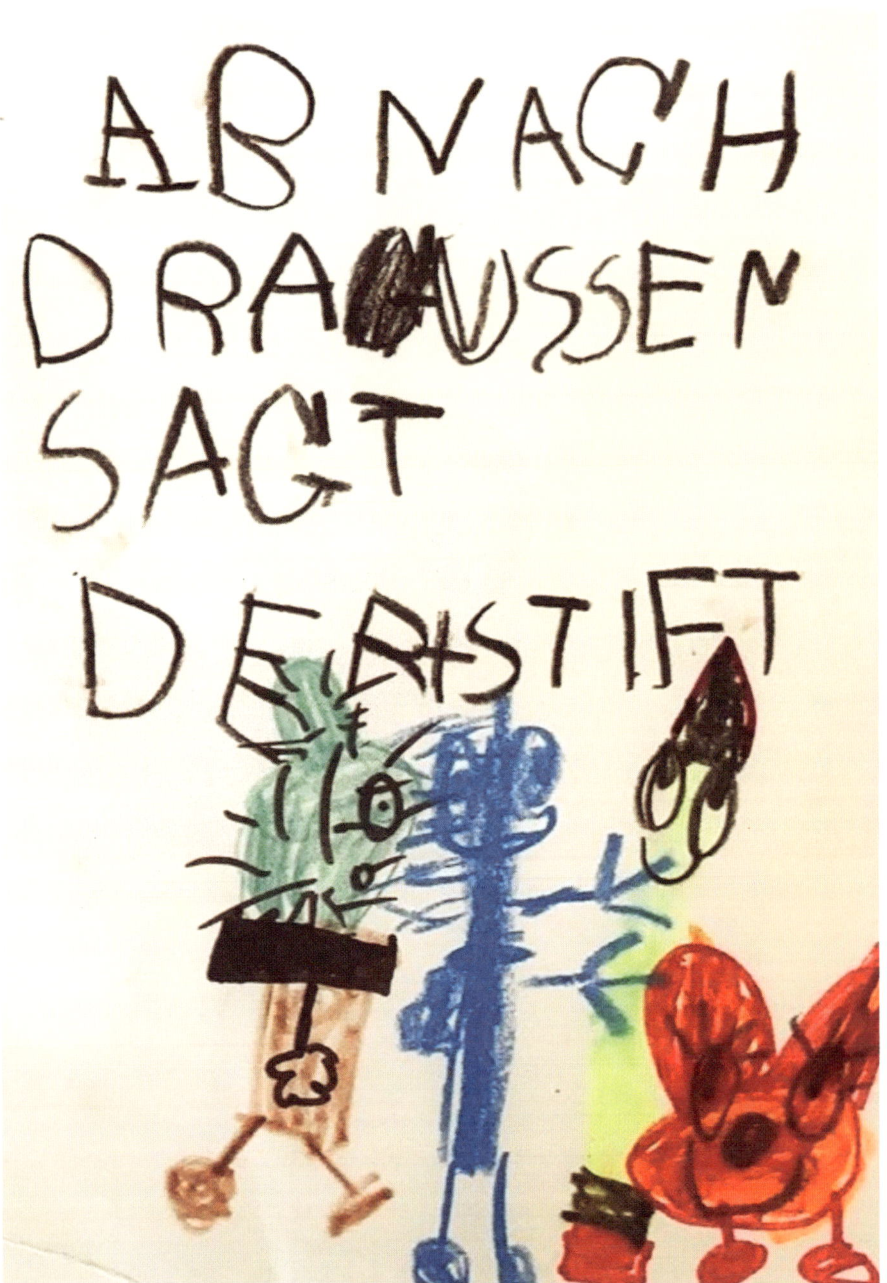

Mari, aged 6, Germany, redesigned book cover. Courtesy Little Museum of Modern Art

LOOKING

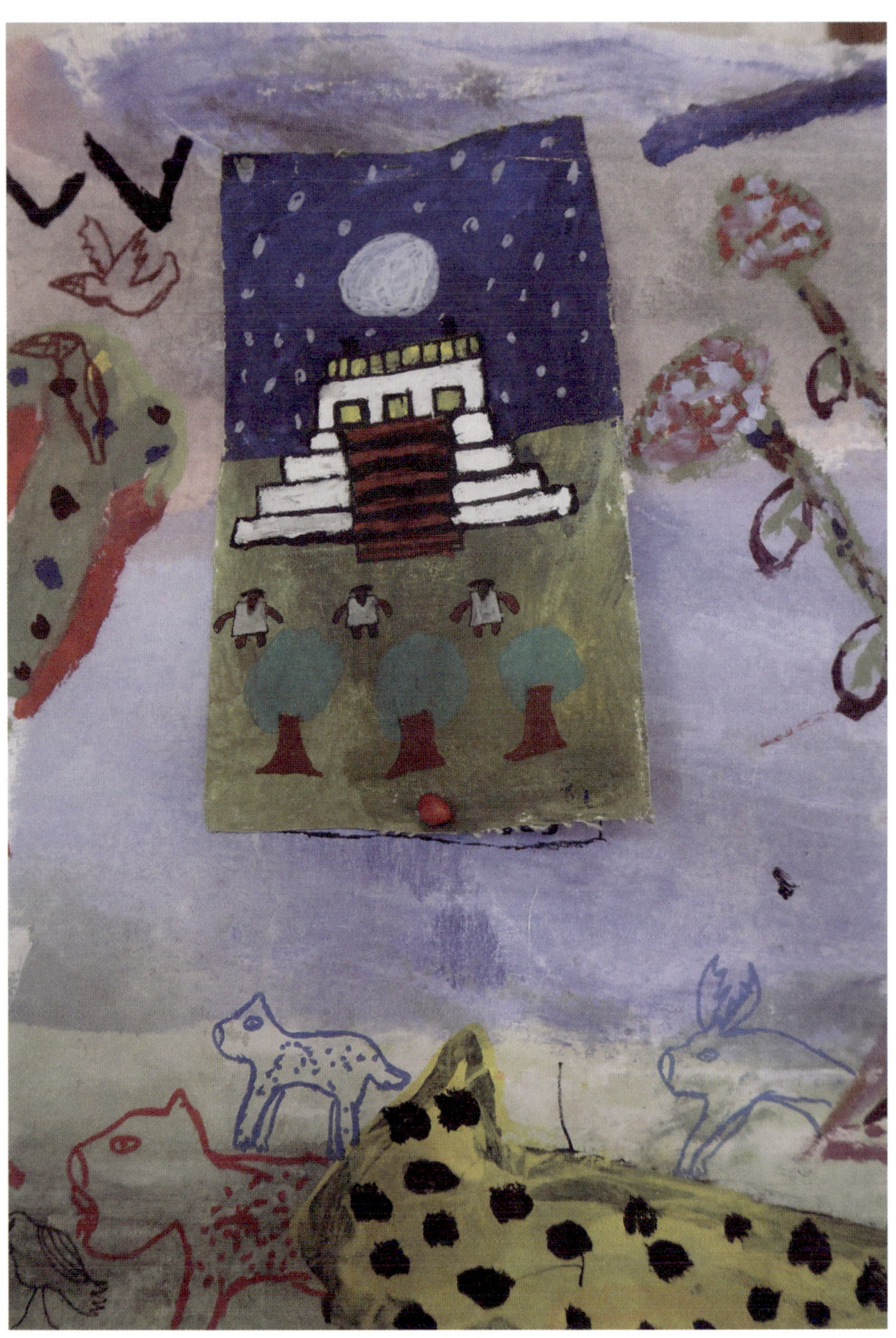

Map of Naha (details of a large mural painted by children which includes a Mayan temple, jaguars, toucans and other creatures), Naha, Chiapas, Mexico, 2016. Courtesy Gill Eatherley

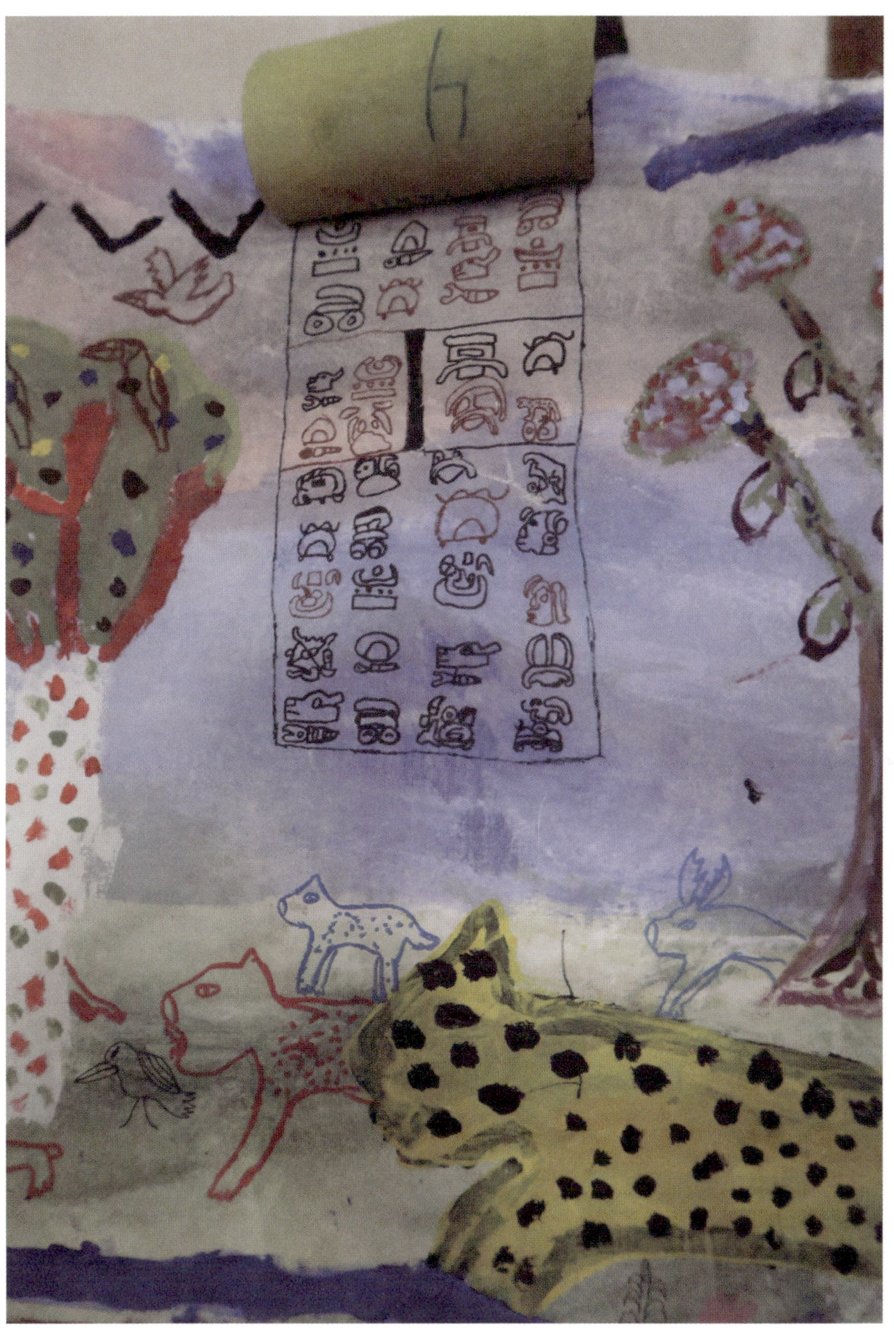

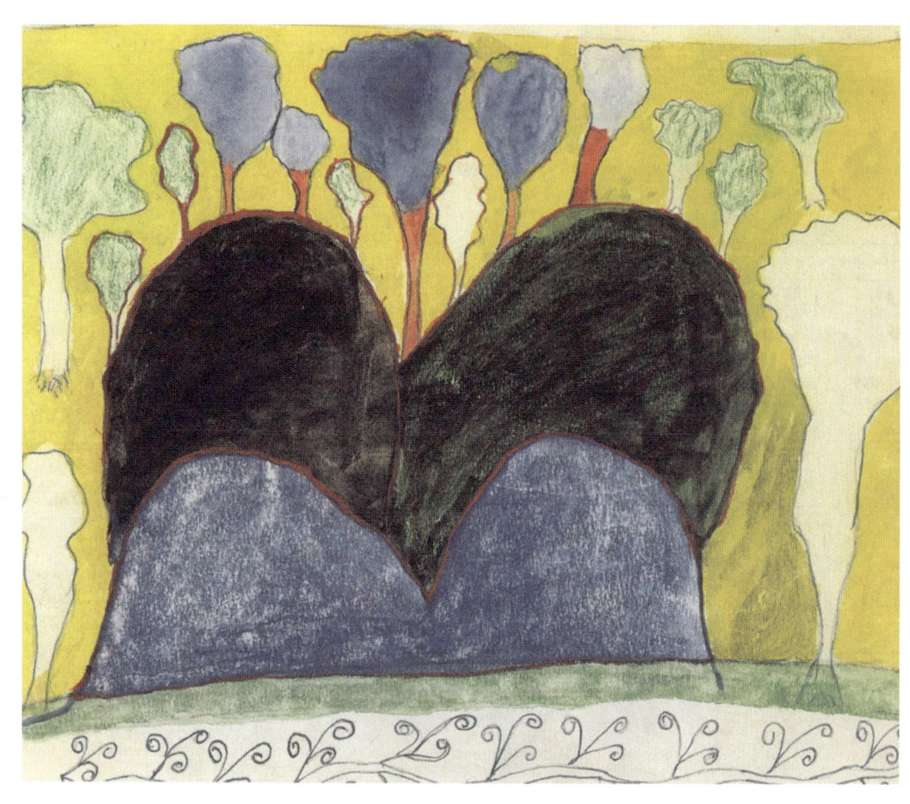

Unknown artist, South Africa, c.1940. From the Cyrene Mission, Zimbabwe

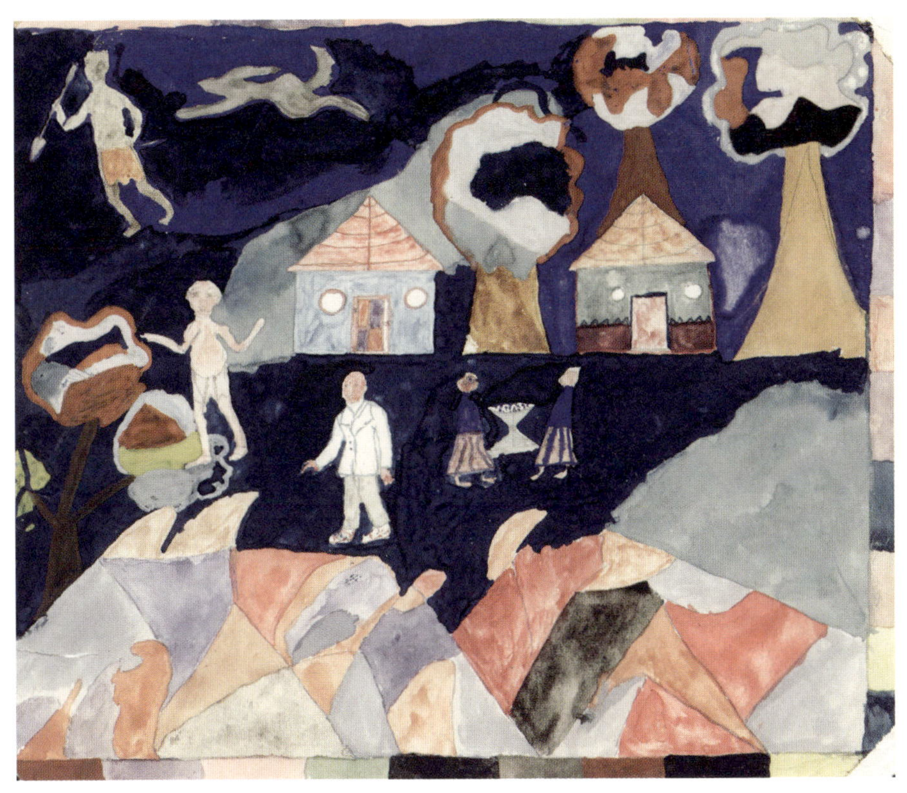

Unknown artist, South Africa, c.1940. From the Cyrene Mission, Zimbabwe

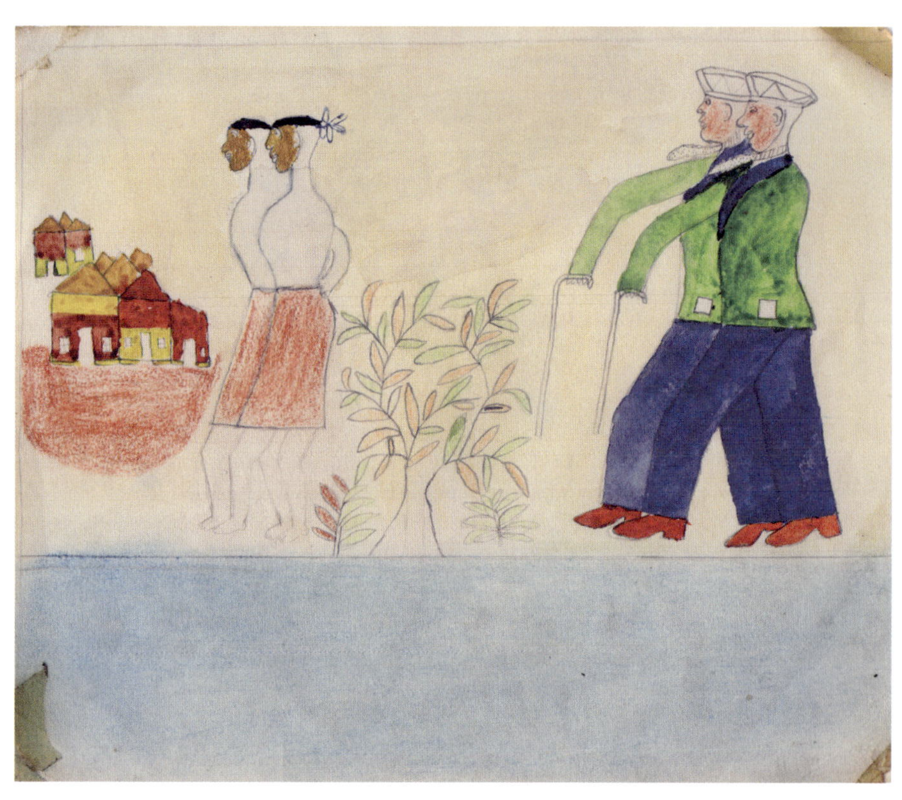

Unknown artist, South Africa, c.1942. From the Cyrene Mission, Zimbabwe

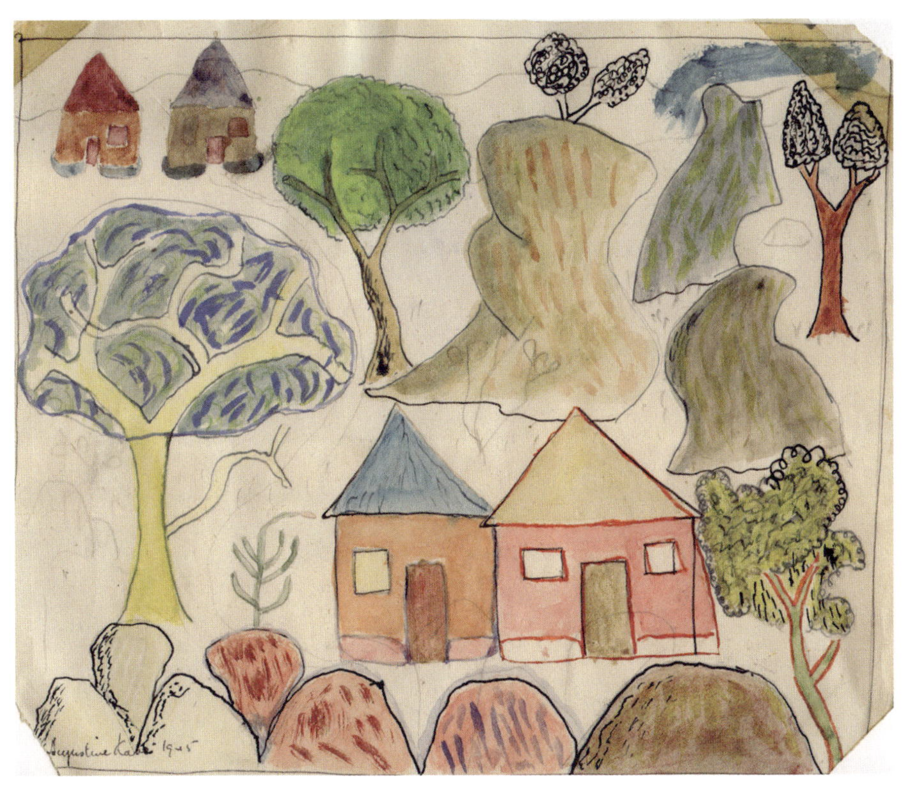

Augustine K., South Africa, 1945. From the Cyrene Mission, Zimbabwe

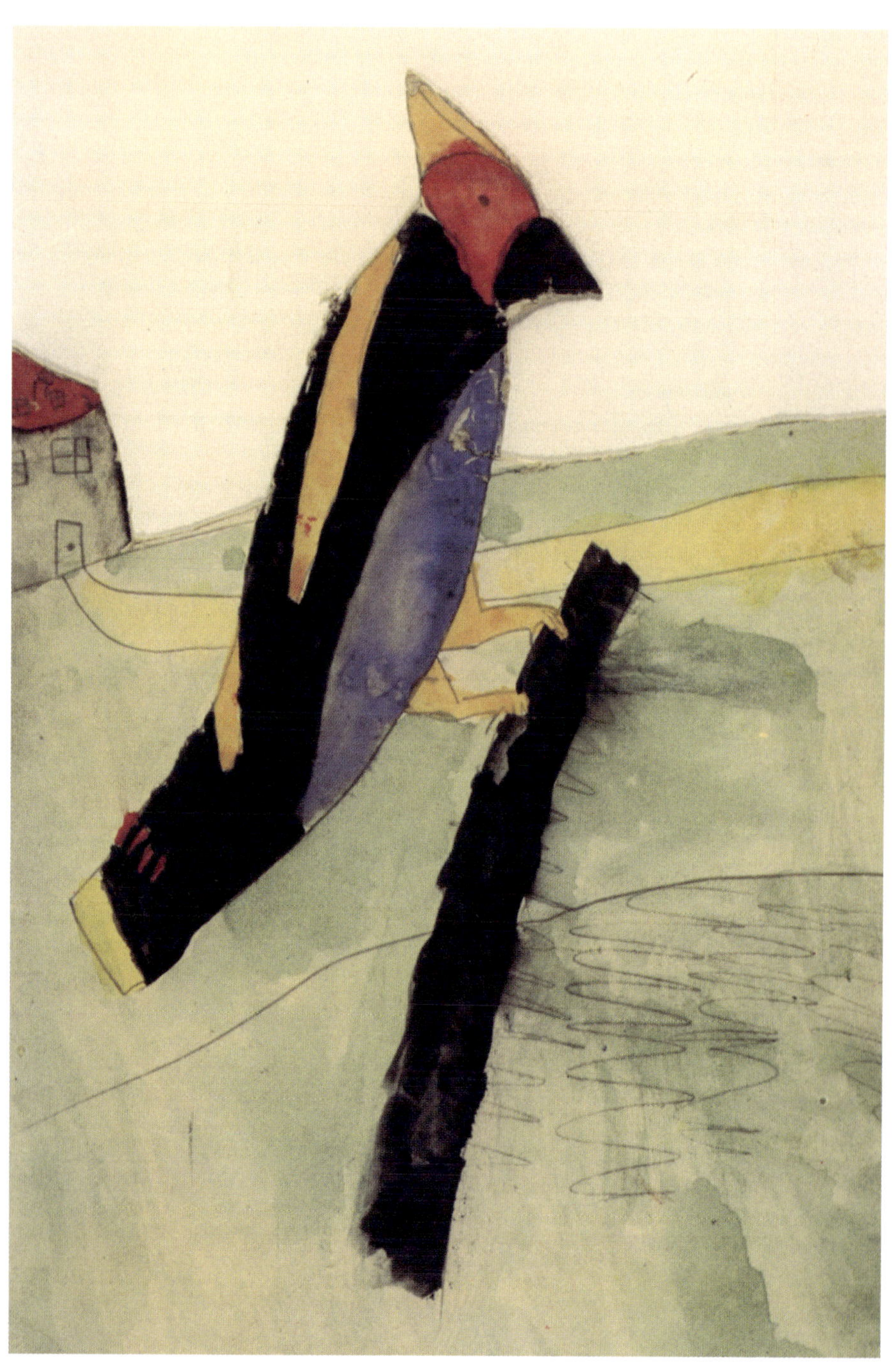

Michael R., aged 9, UK, c.1917

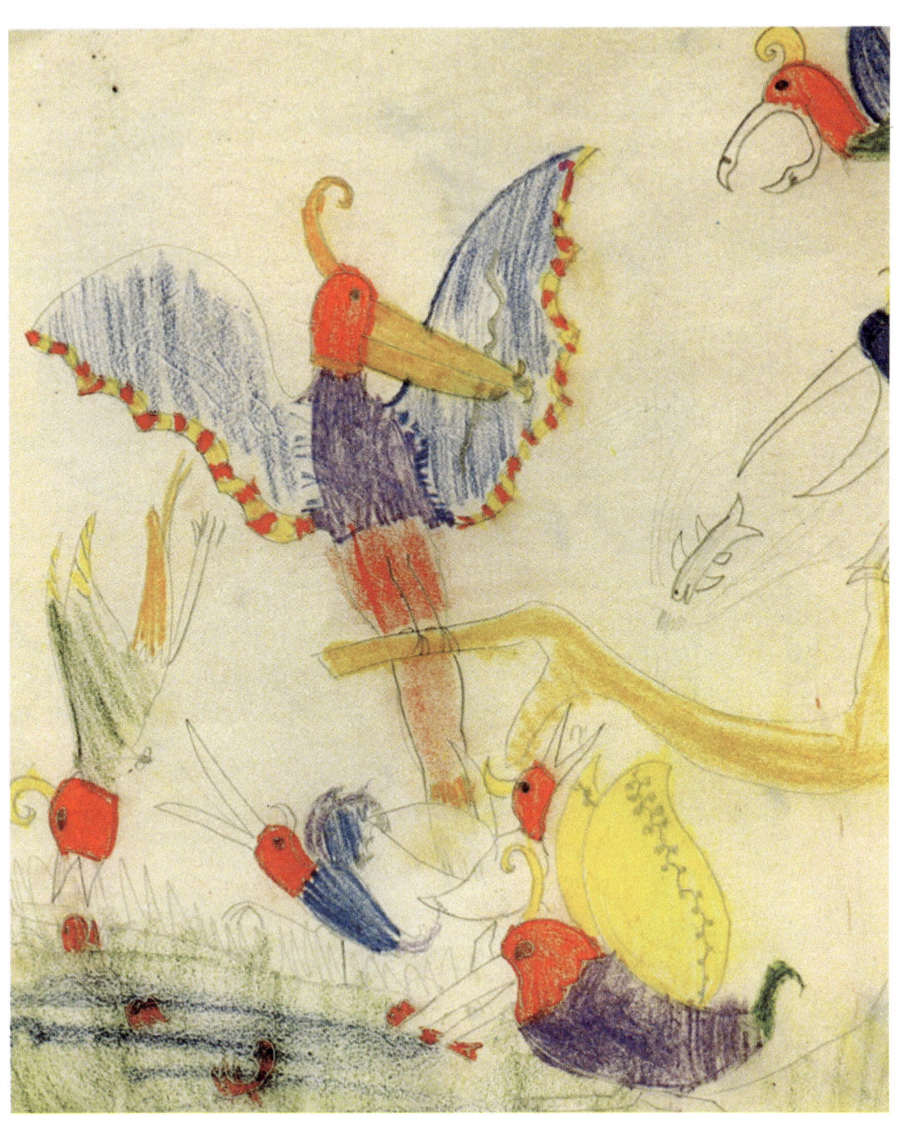

Michael R., aged 9, UK, c.1917

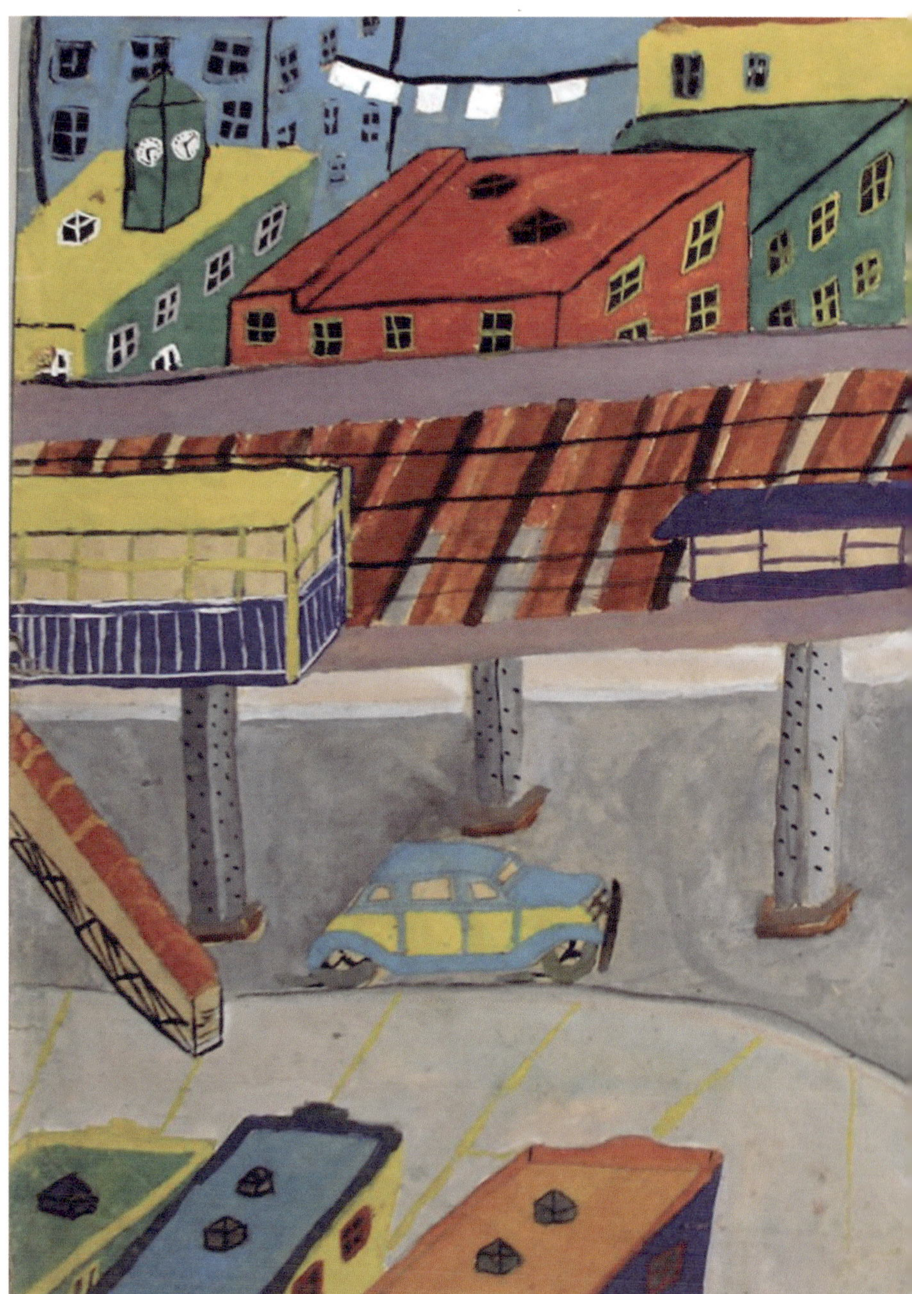

Tony Bonada, aged 12, USA. Courtesy of the Permanent Collection of Children's Museum of the Arts

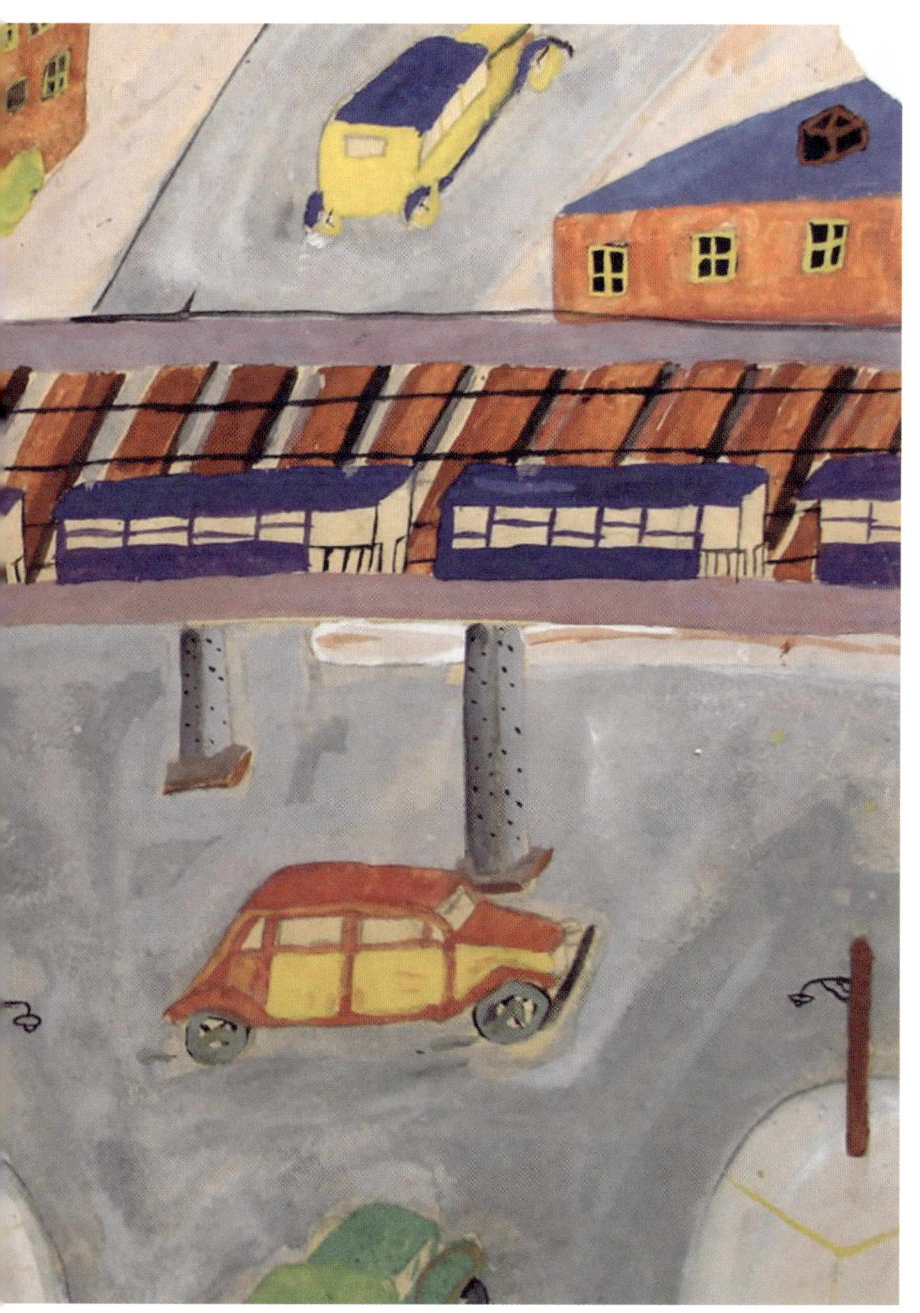

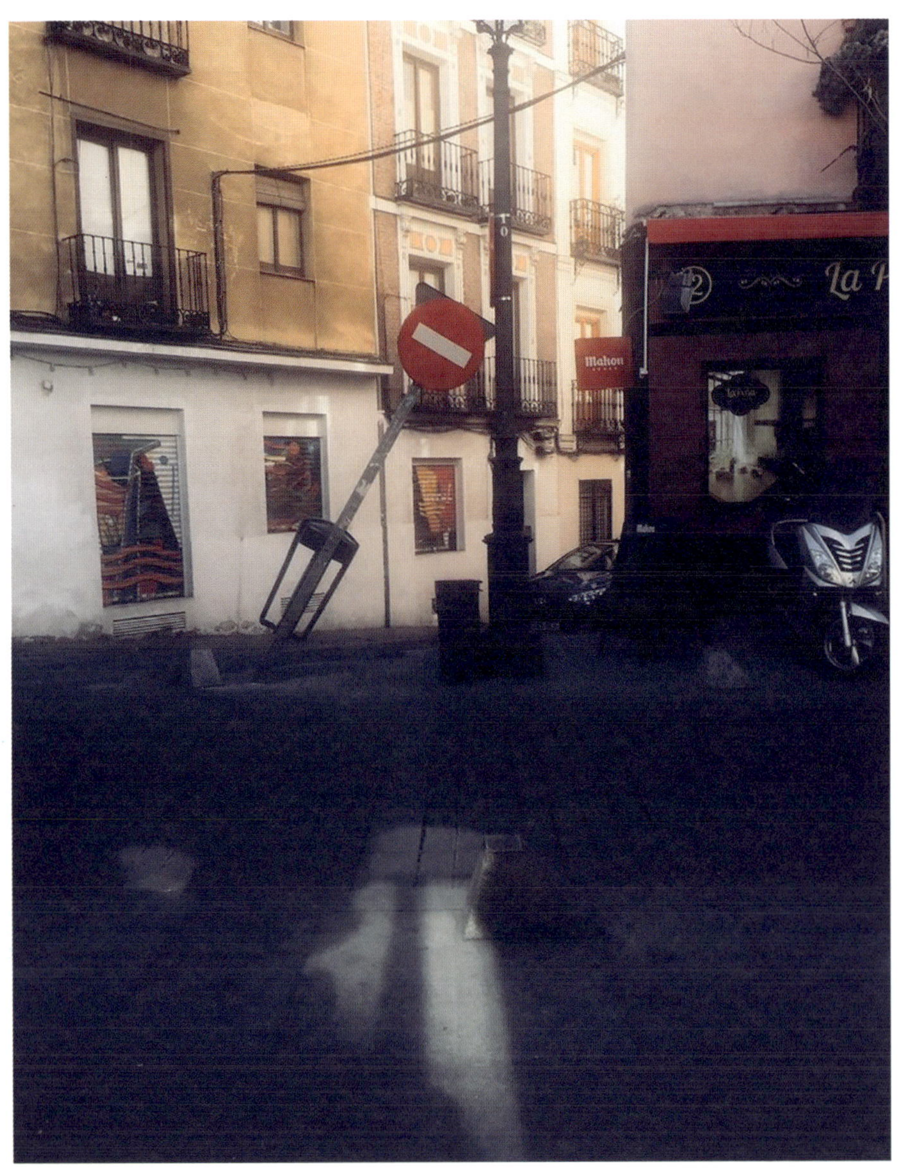

Harriet Waterer, aged 5, Australia

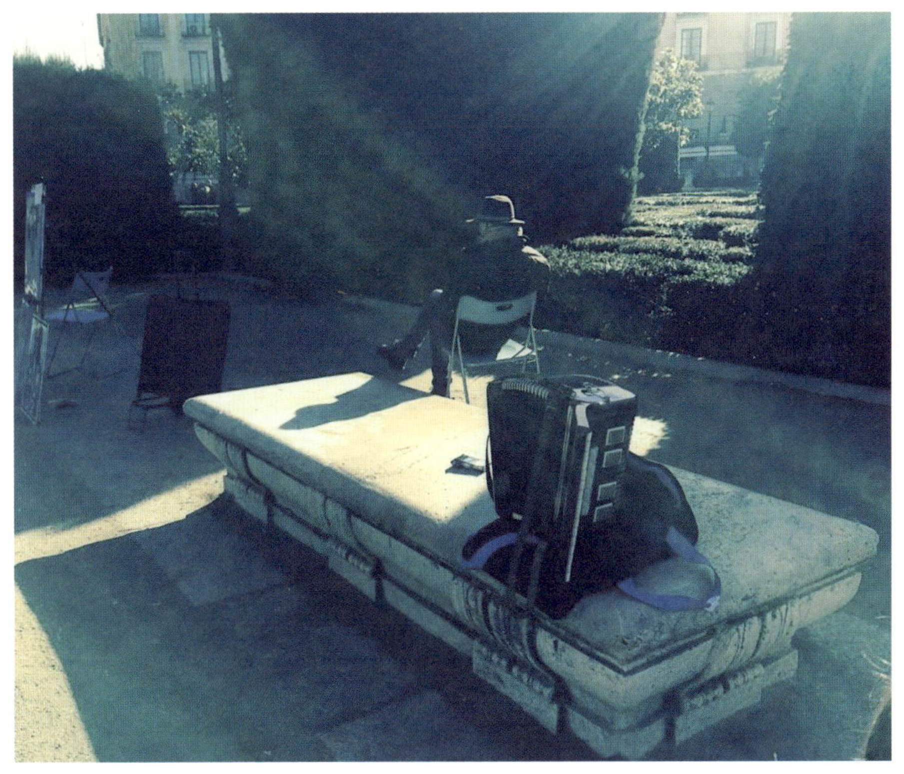

Accordian, Man in Chair, Sunlight, Harriet Waterer, aged 5, Australia

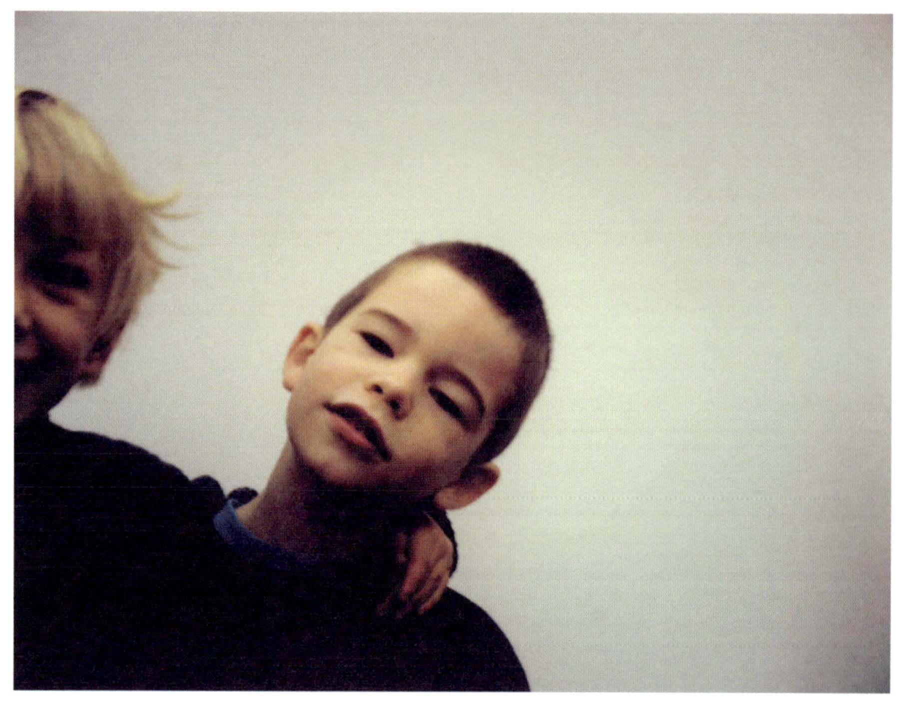

Unknown photographer, aged 7, UK. Courtesy Cubitt Artists

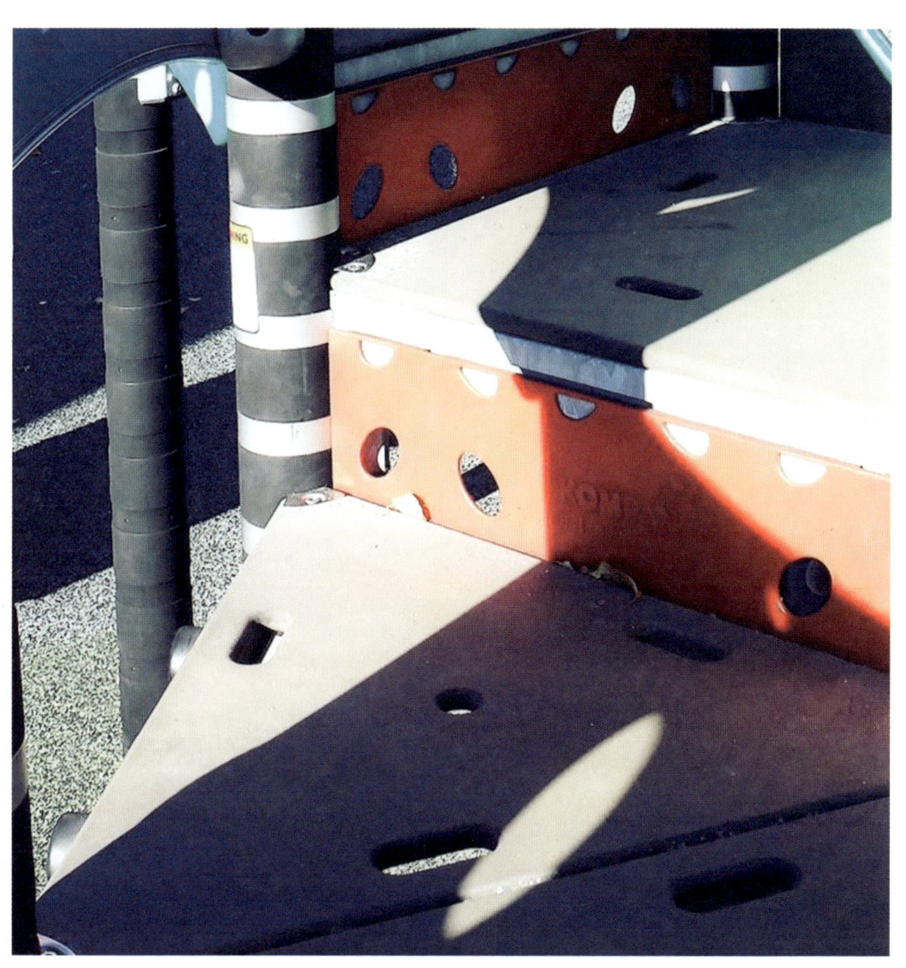

Stairs, unknown photographer, aged 7, UK

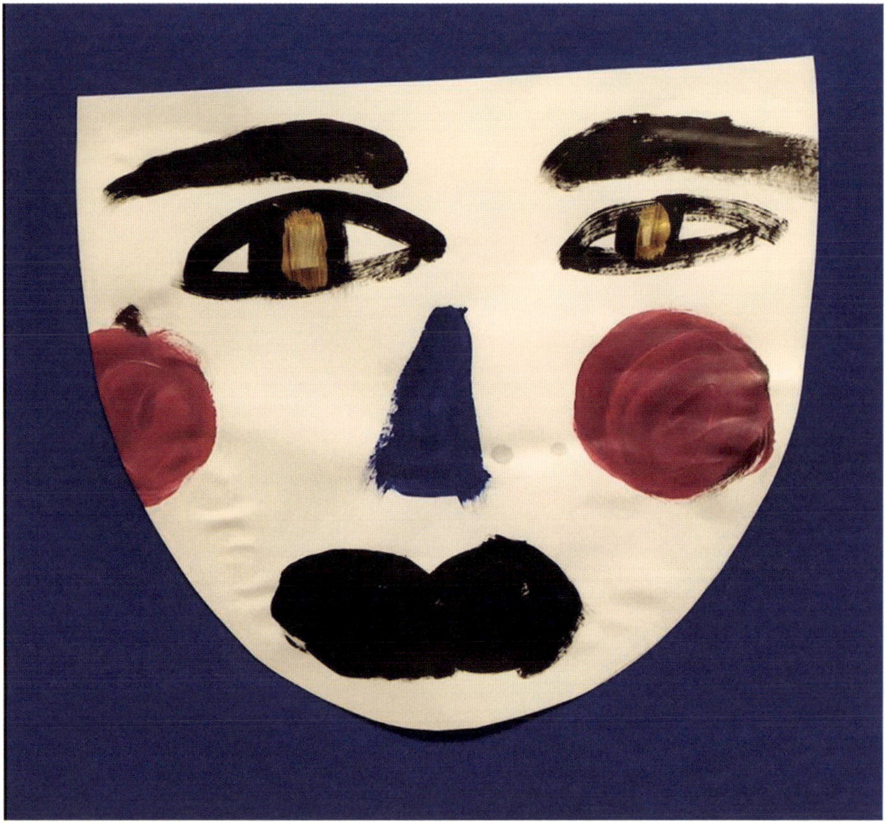

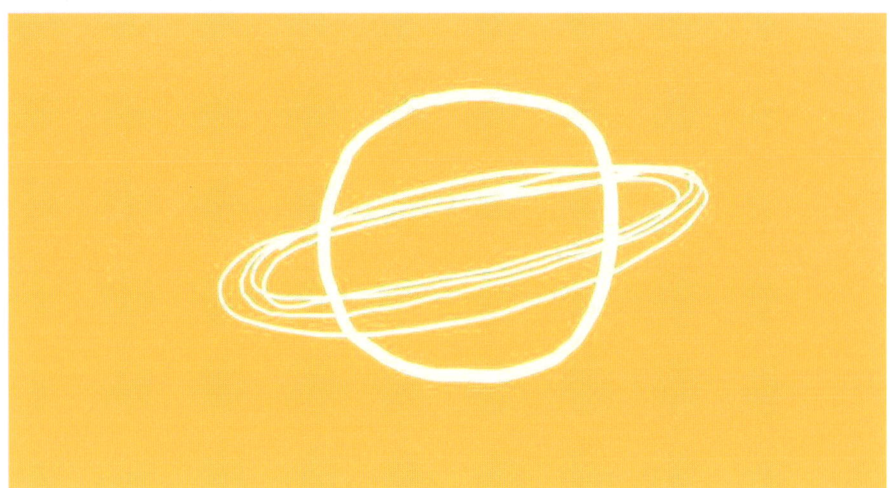

Teka, aged 7, UK

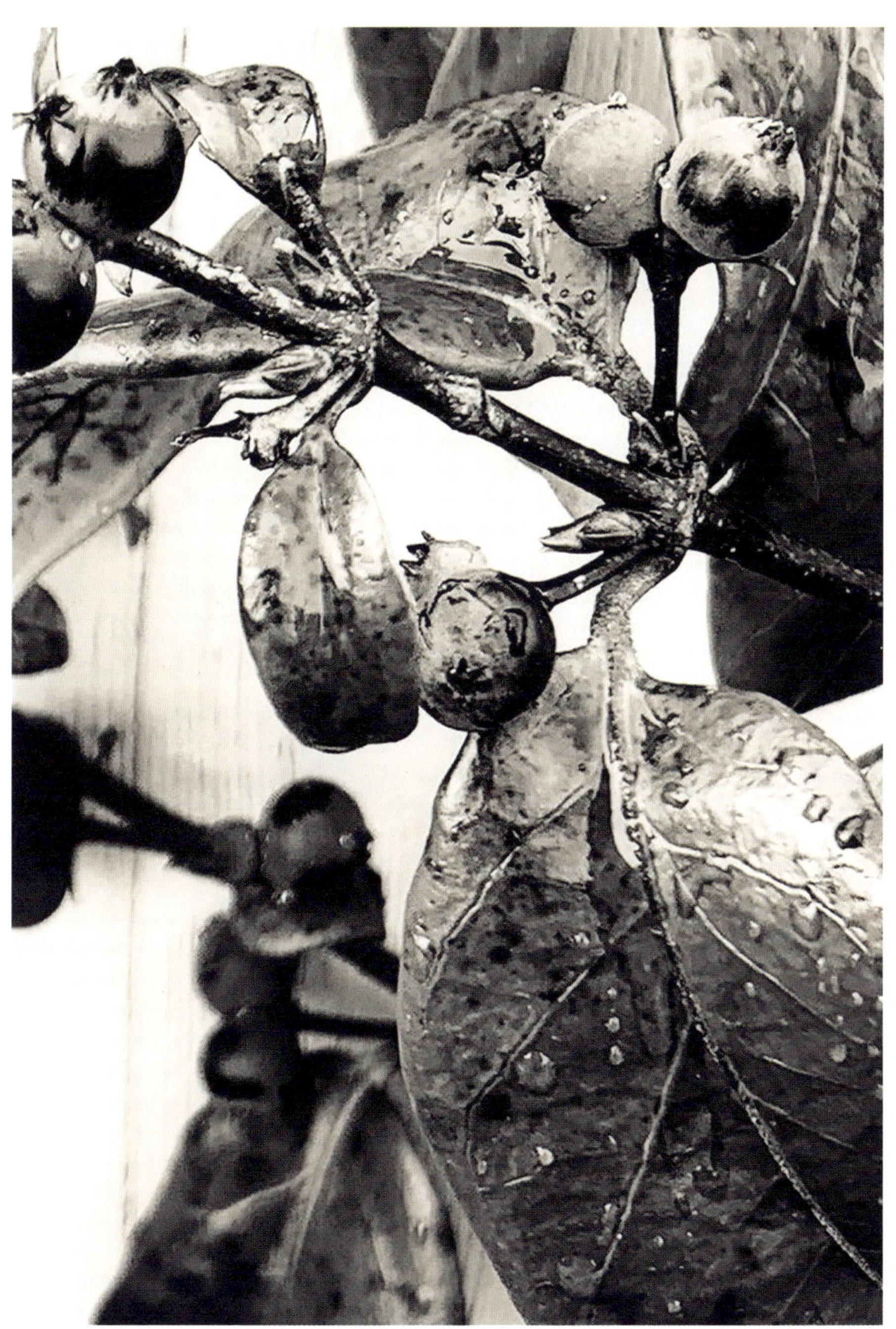

Elisa Hies, aged 9, Germany

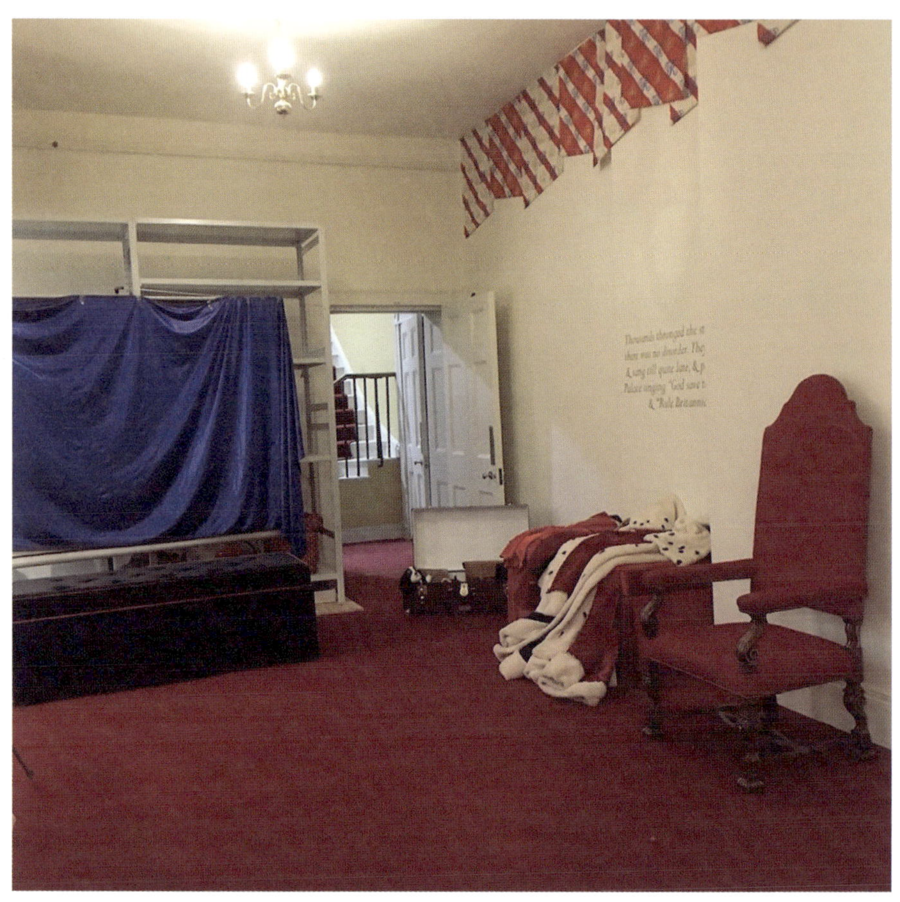

Kensington Palace, unknown photographer, aged 9, UK

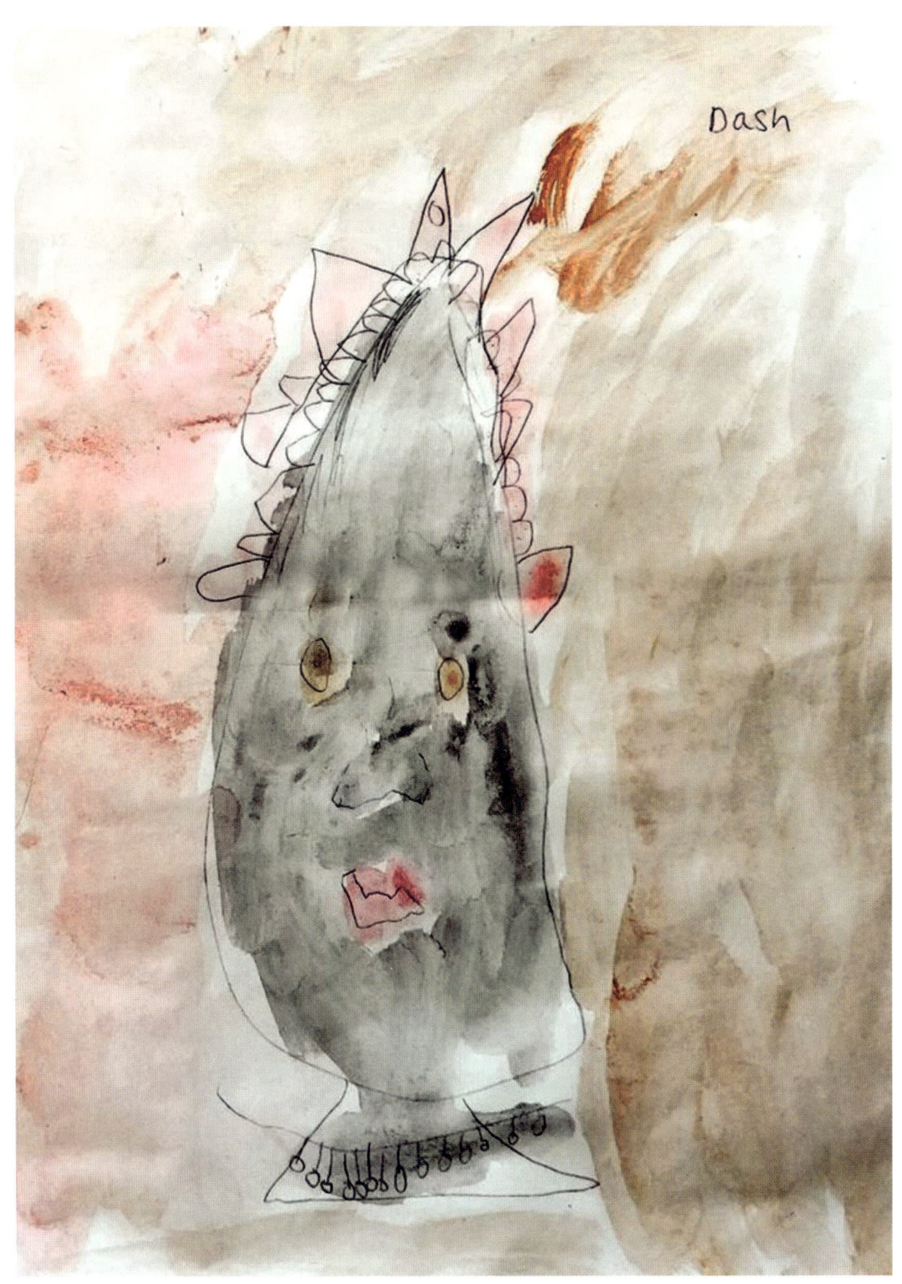

The Queen, Dash Stroud, aged 6, UK

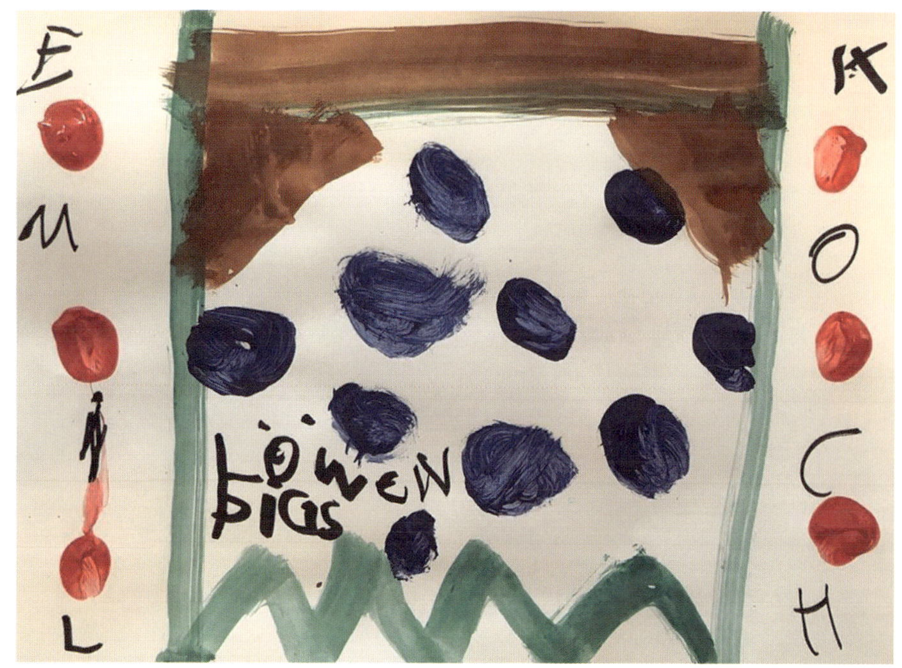

Löwenpigs, Emil, aged 6, Germany

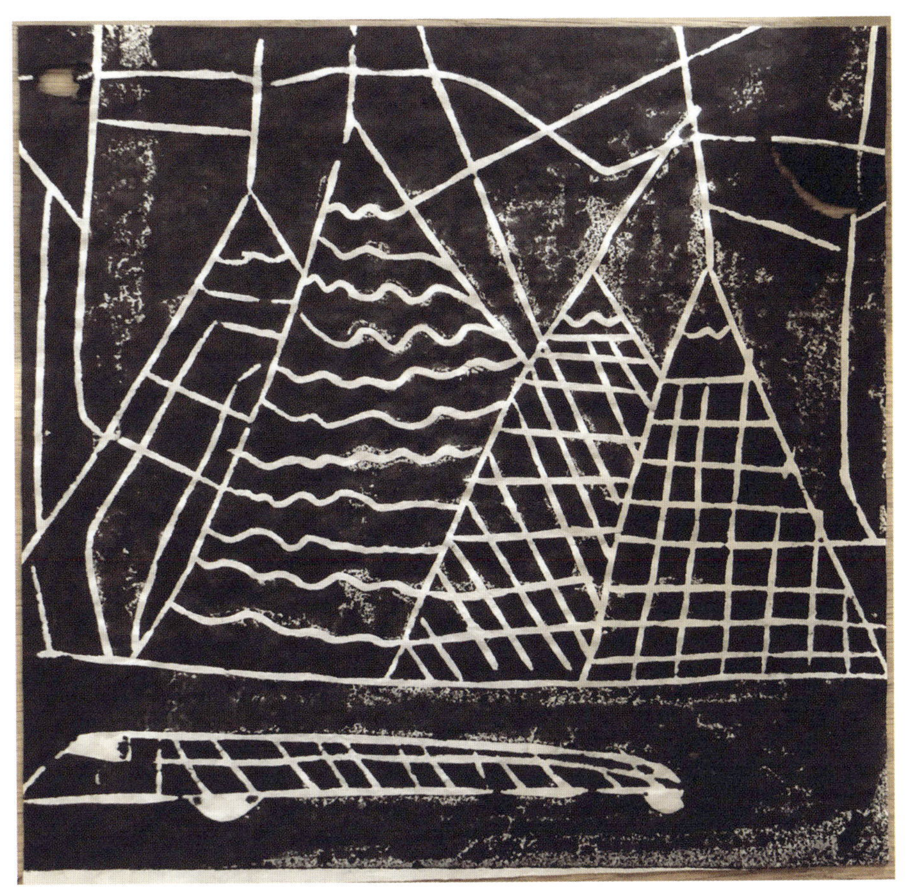

Otto Lowe, aged 9, UK

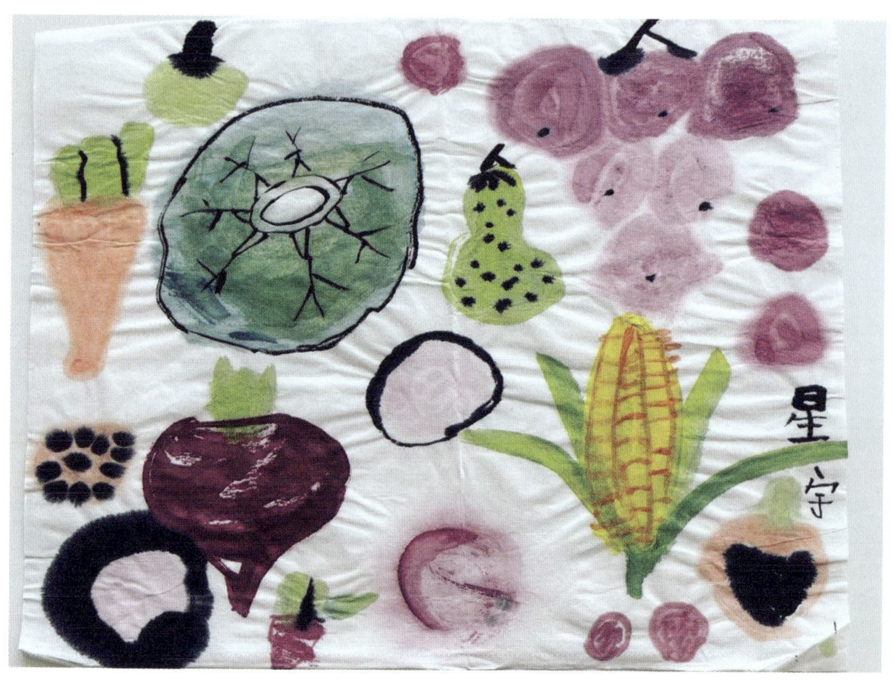

Vegetables, Aidan, aged 5, Japan

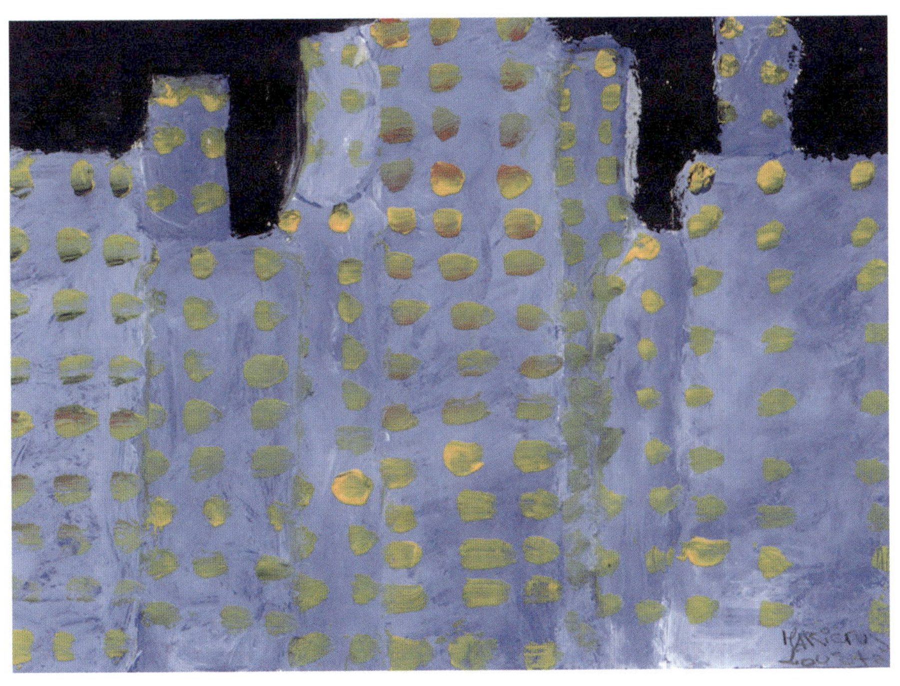

Marie Cruz, *Town at Night*, age unknown, Argentina. Courtesy Constellations.org

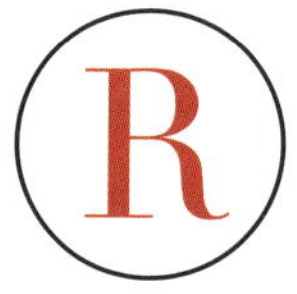

www.theredstoneshop.com